This Is Love

*A Journey Through
the Ten Commandments*

BY STEFANO PIVA

THIS IS LOVE

A JOURNEY THROUGH THE TEN COMMANDMENTS

Belleville, Ontario, Canada

This Is Love
Copyright © 2005, Stefano Piva

All Scripture quotations, unless otherwise specified, are from the *Holy Bible,* New Living Translation, copyright © 1996. Used by permission of Tyndale House Publishers, Inc., Wheaton, IL 60189, USA. All rights reserved.

Library and Archives Canada Cataloguing in Publication

Piva, Stefano, 1973-
　　This is love : a journey through the Ten commandments / Stefano Piva.

Includes bibliographical references.
ISBN 1-55306-855-6

　　1. Ten commandments. I. Title.

BS1285.52.P59 2004　222'.1606　C2004-907147-5

**For more information or
to order additional copies, please contact:**

Stefano Piva
3712-114 Street
Edmonton　AB　T6J 1M1
Canada
stefp@telus.net

Guardian Books is an imprint of *Essence Publishing,* a Christian Book Publisher dedicated to furthering the work of Christ through the written word. For more information, contact:
20 Hanna Court, Belleville, Ontario, Canada K8P 5J2
Phone: 1-800-238-6376 • Fax: (613) 962-3055
E-mail: publishing@essencegroup.com
Internet: www.essencegroup.com

Table of Contents

Acknowledgements

I want to give thanks to God for loving the human race to such an extent that he made the effort to tell us about himself and teach us how to really live. I thank him for the ten commandments, for sending his son Jesus who fulfilled the law and enabled us to have a right relationship with him, and for sending the Holy Spirit so that we could be empowered to really love God and love others and thus truly live by the ten commandments.

Again, as I did in my last book, I would like to thank Greenfield Baptist Church, which continues to be a wonderful community that this pastor finds an honour to shepherd. I especially want to thank my pastoral staff— Les & Cheryl Priebe, Dick Paetzel, Cara Yager, Nona Hait, and Karen Giebelhaus—who are friends more than co-workers. I would like to say a special thanks to Karen Giebelhaus who, once again, read over these chapters and provided me with helpful suggestions, editing, and points of clarification. Without Karen's tireless hours as our church administrator, I wouldn't have had the time to write books such as this. I would also like to say thank you to Dr. Bill Muller and Dr. Dick Paetzel, who have done the same.

Thanks to my wife, Nancy, who reads and edits my work, continually helps me sharpen my ideas, and, at times, patiently listens to me rant! I love you.

I dedicate this book to my two sons, Josiah and Micah. The Lord has called me to *commit* [myself] *wholeheartedly to these commands* [and] *repeat them again and again to* [my] *children.*[1] My hope for the two of you is that you will not only hear me teach these things, but that you will *see* me attempting to live them out before you. My prayer for the two of you is that you will find life in God and his ways, and that you will grow to love and fear him with all your heart, mind, soul, and strength!

---

[1] Deut. 6:4-9.

Introduction

For many people, relativism is absolutely believed. The irony is how few recognize the contradiction. If I believe in an absolute and you disagree with me, that automatically makes you *not* a relativist. Are there really things that are right and things that are wrong, or is it all a matter of personal preference, social conditioning, and upbringing? When a terrorist blows himself up and takes a number of lives with him, can we *judge* that action to be wrong, or is that merely an opinion? If someone else says that a terrorist bombing is right, is that opinion equally valid?[2] In the same way, individuals on both sides of a social issue, such as abortion or homosexuality, argue from what they see as a moral position. Nobody is *really* a relativist. What most

---

[2] I am not denying the fact that certain people do think that terrorist bombings are right and good. The question I am asking is, is there any way to *judge* whether or not the belief that they are holding to is either right or wrong?

self-proclaimed relativists are really saying is, "All things are relative, as long as you agree with me."

In direct opposition to this kind of thinking, we find the God of the Scriptures telling us that certain things are *definitely right* and that others are *definitely wrong*. We find this specifically in the ten commandments[3] that God revealed to Moses and to the nation of Israel, 1200 to 1500 years before Jesus lived on the earth. After Moses went over these commandments with the people he was leading, he said to them:

> *"You must obey all the commands of the LORD your God, following his instructions in every detail. Stay on the path that the LORD your God has commanded you to follow. Then you will live long and prosperous lives in the land you are about to enter and occupy.*
>
> *"Hear, O Israel! The LORD is our God, the LORD alone. And you must love the LORD your God with all your heart, all your soul, and all your strength. And you must commit yourselves wholeheartedly to these commands I am giving you today. Repeat them again and again to your children. Talk about them when you are at home and when you are away on a journey, when you are lying down and when you are getting up again. Tie them to your hands as a reminder, and wear them on your forehead. Write them on the doorposts of your house and on your gates."[4]*

There are a few things that we hear in this summary of the commandments. First, they are for our own good. Obey them and you will "live long and prosper!" As we

---

[3] Exod. 20 & Deut. 5.
[4] Deut. 5:32-33 & 6:4-9.

are going to see throughout this book, God gave us the commandments for our own protection and pleasure.[5] Second, the commandments have something to do with loving God with our whole being, which, in turn, also has something to do with loving one another.[6] This theme will also be followed throughout this book. Third, we are to know and teach these commandments and pass them on to our children, which is why I've dedicated this book to my two sons, Josiah and Micah. The goal of this book is to teach these commandments in light of Christ Jesus, who was the fulfillment of the law.[7] This needs to be done more than ever today, for although the Bible instructs us to live the commandments and teach them in everything we do, my experience has shown that most Christians can't even recite all ten commandments.

So, are there any *universal* standards? God teaches us, through the Bible, that there are. These standards are given to us for our own protection and pleasure. They are given to us so that we will know how to love God and others. They are to be continually taught so that they become a part of us and so that succeeding generations will see and know the ways of the Lord. As John Calvin wrote, "It is vain to attempt new forms of worship to gain the favor of God, whose true worship consists in obedience alone."[8]

---

[5] This is contrary to what many people think. There is a misconception that God gave us these rules to rob us from having an enjoyable life.

[6] See Mark 12:28-34 and the last chapter of this book.

[7] Matt. 5:17.

[8] John Calvin, *Institutes of the Christian Religion,* Book 2, edited and translated by Henry Beveridge (Grand Rapids, MI: Eerdmans, 1997) Chapter 8, Section 5.

CHAPTER ONE

The Purpose of the Commandments

Every sport has rules. Why? The rules are there to make the game interesting, challenging, and to keep the players safe. In other words, the rules are there for the protection and pleasure of the players and the spectators. Anarchy is not only unsafe, but it is also boring. Having no objectives, no purpose, no challenges, no rules, no goals, no winners and no losers means having no fun.

The Ten Commandments

The ten commandments were never meant to repress us but were given for our protection and pleasure. Let's unpack the following truths that the commandments teach us before we look at each one specifically:

1. *The commandments show us God's character.*

2. *The commandments show us how we should live.*

3. *The commandments show us that we are unable to keep them.*

4. *The commandments show us our need for Christ, the fulfillment of the law.*

5. *The commandments show us how God's children live.*

1. The commandments show us God's character.

The Bible teaches us that God is holy,[9] just,[10] faithful,[11] merciful,[12] gracious,[13] and loving.[14] The commandments are based on his character. That is why the Bible says, *"the law itself is holy and right and good."*[15] Therefore, since God is holy, we shouldn't worship anything other than him. Because God is faithful, we shouldn't cheat, and because God is gracious, we shouldn't steal. The law reflects his character.

2. The commandments show us how we should live.

The commandments are part of the moral fabric that holds our world together. The commandments are natural laws, and when we break them we rebel against God's original intent for creation. All the destruction, decay, and death we see around us are a result of God's natural commands being broken. Paul writes in Romans: *"For all creation is waiting eagerly for that future day when God will reveal who his children really are. Against its will, everything on earth was subjected to God's curse."*[16]

---

[9] Lev. 19:2, Is. 6:3.

[10] Deut. 32:4.

[11] 2 Tim. 2:13.

[12] Ps. 145:9.

[13] Exod. 34:6-7.

[14] 1 John 4:8.

[15] Rom. 7:12.

[16] Rom. 8:19-20.

When God originally created, he declared *all* of his creation *very good*.[17] Due to disobedience, however, the whole world was subjected to death.[18] God is life and the life giver.[19] If the commandments are based on God's character and God is the very source from which life comes, then the commandments show us how to live. On the other hand, when we disobey the commandments, we really rebel against God's character, and the consequences of disobeying the source of life is death. A society of individuals who kill, steal, lie, and cheat will not live long. The ten commandments are based on God's character, and because God stamped his character into his creation, the ten commandments are natural laws that teach us the way things work. That is why Paul could write these words of people who had never seen the commandments before:

> *Even when Gentiles, who do not have God's written law, instinctively follow what the law says, they show that in their hearts they know right from wrong. They demonstrate that God's law is written within them, for their own consciences either accuse them or tell them they are doing what is right.*[20]

3. The commandments show us that we are unable to keep them.

There is a problem with what has been said so far. For even though the commandments show us God's character and show us what is natural to creation, we are unable to

---

[17] Gen. 1:31.

[18] Gen. 3:17-19.

[19] Gen. 2:7.

[20] Rom. 2:14-15.

maintain obedience to them—especially, as we will see, in light of the tenth commandment. Again, Paul writes:

> *For no one can ever be made right in God's sight by doing what his law commands. For the more we know God's law, the clearer it becomes that we aren't obeying it.*[21]
>
> *But those who depend on the law to make them right with God are under his curse, for the Scriptures say, "Cursed is everyone who does not observe and obey all these commands that are written in God's Book of the Law." Consequently, it is clear that no one can ever be right with God by trying to keep the law.*[22]

John Calvin admitted that at times it seemed as if "God wanted to mock (people) in his law in that he almost forbade them to scratch themselves after making (them) itch."[23] Something has gone wrong, and that something is disobedience. All of us in Adam and Eve sinned against God and his way. This made things abnormal. Sin became a scar on our humanity[24] and upon creation. In fact, whenever someone says that something is *wrong* they are alluding to a standard, a person, or a time when things were right. Because we know that the commandments are our guides to life but we are not able to keep them, they reveal to us that we need help. We read in the Bible:

---

[21] Rom. 3:20.

[22] Gal. 3:10-11.

[23] John Calvin, *Ten Commandments*, Edited and translated by Benjamin Farley (Grand Rapids, MI: Baker, 1980) p. 277.

[24] We don't sin because we are human but because we are damaged humans.

16

Did the law, which is good, cause my doom? Of course not! Sin used what was good to bring about my condemnation. So we can see how terrible sin really is. It uses God's good commandment for its own evil purposes.[25]

By not being able to keep the law, the law revealed to us our need for a saviour. This leads to the fourth point.

4. The commandments show us our need for Christ, the fulfillment of the law.

Jesus said, *"Don't misunderstand why I have come. I did not come to abolish the law of Moses or the writings of the prophets. No, I came to fulfill them."*[26] How did Jesus do this? Jesus did this by becoming a human being and, though he *"faced all of the same temptations we do, yet he did not sin."*[27] We face temptation and fail, and we bring upon ourselves a curse. *"Cursed is anyone who does not affirm the terms of this law by obeying them."*[28] Jesus, however, never sinned, and yet he chose to take our curse upon himself when he gave up his life on the cross. That is why Paul wrote:

But Christ has rescued us from the curse pronounced by the law. When he was hung on the cross, he took upon himself the curse for our wrongdoing. For it is written in the Scriptures, "Cursed is everyone who is hung on a tree."[29]

---

[25] Rom. 7:13.

[26] Matt. 5:17.

[27] Heb. 4:15.

[28] Deut. 27:26.

[29] Gal. 3:13.

This is why John the Baptist said of Jesus, *"Look! There is the Lamb of God who takes away the sin of the world!"*[30]

Jesus fulfilled the law in that he never broke any of the commandments. He perfectly obeyed his Heavenly Father. He also fulfilled the consequences of disobedience to the law by taking upon himself our sin and our punishment. Therefore, salvation comes not by obeying the law, which no one can do, but through faith in Christ and what he did on our behalf. *"Consequently, it is clear that no one can ever be right with God by trying to keep the law. For the Scriptures say, 'It is through faith that a righteous person has life.'"*[31] Notice that it says "through faith a righteous person has *life*." This is because Jesus not only died for our sins and offered us forgiveness, but he rose from the dead—showing that he is more powerful than death—and offered us life.

When we surrender ourselves to him, Jesus points us back to the rules of life. Jesus said, *"If you love me, obey my commandments."*[32] So we have come full circle, with one major difference, as we will see in the fifth point.

5. The commandments show us how God's children live.

The major difference regarding the commandments for those in Christ, as opposed to those outside of Christ, is that they are now empowered to live according to God's character and rules. Paul wrote:

> *Those who are dominated by the sinful nature think about sinful things, but those who are controlled by the*

---

[30] John 1:29.

[31] Gal. 3:11.

[32] John 14:15.

Holy Spirit think about things that please the Spirit. If your sinful nature controls your mind, there is death. But if the Holy Spirit controls your mind, there is life and peace. For the sinful nature is always hostile to God. It never did obey God's laws, and it never will. That's why those who are still under the control of their sinful nature can never please God.

But you are not controlled by your sinful nature. You are controlled by the Spirit if you have the Spirit of God living in you. (And remember that those who do not have the Spirit of Christ living in them are not Christians at all.) Since Christ lives within you, even though your body will die because of sin, your spirit is alive because you have been made right with God. The Spirit of God, who raised Jesus from the dead, lives in you. And just as he raised Christ from the dead, he will give life to your mortal body by this same Spirit living within you.[33]

Through the power of the Holy Spirit, Christians have been empowered to live as God called them to live. We Christians are not perfect yet, but as we learn to walk with the Spirit and surrender our will to the Spirit, we are being transformed and made new, so that on the Day of Resurrection[34] we will all be transformed to perfection in the blinking of an eye.[35]

As we open our hearts to the work of the Spirit, let us walk through these ten commandments—no matter how uncomfortable it may be at times—and allow him to shape

---

[33] Rom. 8:5-11.

[34] 1 Thess. 4:13-18.

[35] 1 Cor. 15:51-52.

"a spiritual renewal of [our] *thoughts and attitudes.* [We] *must display a new nature because* [we] *are a new person, created in God's likeness—righteous, holy, and true."*[36]

---

[36] Eph. 4:23-24.

CHAPTER TWO
I'm Number One

*I am the L*ORD *your God, who*
rescued you from slavery in Egypt.
Do not worship any other gods besides me. [37]

Wayne Gretzky was number one when it came to playing hockey. The Beatles used to be the number one rock band in the world, and some would claim that they still are. When it comes to making money, many would say that Bill Gates is number one. The civilization of Rome was number one until the barbarians sacked it. Today, many see America as number one. At the time of this writing, the United Nations has deemed Canada the number one place in the world to live.

Some people think Coke is number one. Others think Pepsi is number one. Some people think that they are number one. In fact, the Egyptian Pharaoh Amenhetep III (1401-1364 B.C.) was so convinced that he was number one that he ordered his stonecutters to chisel out a picture of himself worshipping himself. [38] The Pharaoh that Moses dealt with also thought that he was number

---

[37] Deut. 5:6-7.

[38] E.A.W. Budge, *Tutankhamen* (New York, NY: Bell) p. 26.

one, until he played chess with God and lost. [39]

Many "number ones" come and many "number ones" go, but eventually, as the Bible says:

> *The hot sun rises and dries up the grass; the flower withers, and its beauty fades away. So also, wealthy people will fade away with all of their achievements.* [40]

Job was correct when he said:

> *"I came naked from my mother's womb, and I will be stripped of everything when I die. The LORD gave me everything I had, and the LORD has taken it away. Praise the name of the LORD!"* [41]

Is Anyone Number One?

There is someone who has been number one and who will always be number one, without beginning or end. As already mentioned, the Pharaoh of the Exodus met him and rebelled against him—whereas Moses submitted to him. At the end of the Exodus story, it was not so much about Pharaoh or Moses but about whose side they were on. When Moses first encountered Number One and was given an assignment by him, he asked:

> *"If I go to the people of Israel and tell them, 'The God of your ancestors has sent me to you,' they won't believe me. They will ask, 'Which god are you talking about? What is his name?' Then what should I tell them?"*
>
> *God replied, "I Am the One Who Always Is. Just*

---

[39] See Exodus 1-20.

[40] Jas. 1:11.

[41] Job 1:21.

*tell them, 'I Am has sent me to you.' " God also said,
"Tell them, 'The LORD, the God of your ancestors—the
God of Abraham, the God of Isaac, and the God of
Jacob—has sent me to you.' This will be my name for-
ever; it has always been my name, and it will be used
throughout all generations."*[42]

God is number one! Not just any god, but the God of
Abraham, Isaac, and Jacob. This same God later gave his
ten commandments to Moses and stated his position as
number one in the very first command.

*"I am the LORD your God, who rescued you from slavery
in Egypt. Do not worship any other gods besides me."*[37]

God is clearly saying in the first commandment, "I'm
number one!"

Is God Arrogant?

Some think that this is quite arrogant of God, to say that
he is number one. The Bible, however, says that *"the LORD is
a jealous God, filled with vengeance and wrath. He takes revenge
on all who oppose him and furiously destroys his enemies!"*[43]
So why does God steal all the glory? Why doesn't he
realize that other religions also have their gods? Most
branches of Hinduism have thousands of gods.
Why doesn't the God of Abraham, Isaac, and Jacob learn
to share his glory a little? Let me give you three reasons.

1. The God of the Bible is the only real God.

A few years back an article in *Newsweek* described this

---

[42] Exod. 3:13-15.
[43] Nahum 1:2.

popular trend of people worshipping their own projected ideas.[44] The article was entitled "Searching for a Holy Spirit," and the subtitle stated "Young people are openly passionate about religion—but they insist on defining it in their own way." When asked their thoughts about God, the following statements were made: "He is like a grandfather." "He is an evil being who wants to punish me all the time." "I believe that there is a higher power at work in my life, but I do not have a name for it." "When I pray I do not ask a god to make everything all right. Instead I ask myself to be strong." The one statement that almost all respondents agreed upon was "God is whatever works for you."[45]

This first commandment does not deny that people worship all kinds of different things besides the true God. Even if they do not overtly call the object or being of their worship a *god*, they still treat it as one. People worship pleasure, money, family, church, sex, celebrities, food, and a host of other things. None of those things, however, are the *real* God. They may be good things, but when they become the object of our greatest devotion they will fail us, because they are not able to fill the role of God. Because God knows that all of these things are false gods, he tells us "I'm number one," not out of arrogance but as simple

---

[44] This was the criticism that men like Feuerbach, Marx, Freud and Nietzsche made about Christians. As Christians we also can project our own ideas onto the God of the Bible and then claim to worship or reject him. Is the God you are worshipping or rejecting the *real* God revealed in the Scriptures? This is a question we all need to ask ourselves.

[45] John Leland, "Searching for a Holy Spirit: Young people are openly passionate about religion—but they insist on defining it in their own way," *Newsweek*, May 8, 2000.

truth. God tells us this for our own protection and pleasure, in order to save us from futile attempts to make untruths into truths. God cannot share his glory because that would make God a liar. He is the only one who is all-powerful. He is the only one who has always existed. He is the only one who knows all things. He is the only one who has created all things out of nothing. I could go on, but the point has been made. God cannot share his glory because to do that would not be true to reality.

False gods have no ability to reach us or fill our emptiness. In fact, false gods are often just an extended worship of our own ideas. Trying to help ourselves by worshipping a self-created false god is like trying to pull on your left hand with your right hand in an attempt to pull yourself up a cliff. You are not going to make it to the top unless someone other than yourself who is already at the top reaches down his or her hand, grabs your hand, and you allow him or her to pull you up. It is not arrogant for that person to tell you that he or she is on the top. That person *is* on the top!

No Excuses

In the first commandment, God says that nothing in our lives should come before him, because the reality is that nothing is greater than him. Paul writes that our individualistic and rebellious nature tries to suppress this truth:

> *From the time the world was created, people have seen the earth and sky and all that God made. They can clearly see his invisible qualities—his eternal power and divine nature. So they have no excuse whatsoever for not knowing God.*

Yes, they knew God, but they wouldn't worship him as God or even give him thanks. And they began to think up foolish ideas of what God was like. The result was that their minds became dark and confused. Claiming to be wise, they became utter fools instead. And instead of worshiping the glorious, ever-living God, they worshiped idols made to look like mere people, or birds and animals and snakes.[46]

2. The God of the Bible is the only God who himself rescued humanity.

The second reason that God can give a first commandment that says he is number one is because he did *all* the work in saving us. This is even stated as a reason in the first commandment: *"I am the LORD your God, who rescued you from slavery in Egypt,"* therefore *"do not worship any gods before me."*

Now you might be thinking, "But I was never a slave in Egypt. In fact, I've never been to Egypt." That may be true in a physical sense, but not in a spiritual sense. What happened to Israel physically was a picture of what has also happened to humanity spiritually. We were all born as slaves to a sinful nature. That is why we suppress the truth of the reality of God being number one. Israel's enslavement in Egypt is a symbol of our life of bondage to our passions, whims, and desires; but just as God set Israel free from the Egyptians, so we have been set free from our slavery. God *has* reached down his hand and is able to pull us up if we will grab onto him. How can this happen? The Apostle John wrote: *"For God so loved the world that he gave*

---

[46] Rom. 1:20-23.

*his only Son, so that everyone who believes in him will not
perish but have eternal life.*[47]

Through Christ Jesus, God rescued us. As Paul wrote
to the Romans:

> *For all have sinned; all fall short of God's glorious stan-
> dard. Yet now God in his gracious kindness declares us
> not guilty. He has done this through Christ Jesus, who
> has freed us by taking away our sins.*[48]
>
> *Now you are free from the power of sin and have
> become slaves of God. Now you do those things that lead
> to holiness and result in eternal life. For the wages of sin
> is death, but the free gift of God is eternal life through
> Christ Jesus our Lord.*[49]

3. The God of the Bible is the only one to have conquered sin and death.

The third reason that God can claim to be number one
has to do with how he went about gaining our freedom.
The God who told Moses that his name was "I AM" is the
same God that Jesus claimed to be.[50] We can be set free
from our bondage, sin, and death because God, through
Christ, saved us.

> *Your attitude should be the same that Christ Jesus had.
> Though he was God, he did not demand and cling to his*

---

[47] John 3:16.

[48] Rom. 3:23-24.

[49] Rom. 6:23-24.

[50] i.e. John 8:54-59; John 1:1-5, 14; Col. 1:15-20; Phil. 2:5-11; Heb. 1.
Also see my book *All Roads Lead Somewhere* for a more thorough
look at the person of Christ and the doctrine of the Trinity.

rights as God. He made himself nothing; he took the humble position of a slave and appeared in human form. And in human form he obediently humbled himself even further by dying a criminal's death on a cross. Because of this, God raised him up to the heights of heaven and gave him a name that is above every other name, so that at the name of Jesus every knee will bow, in heaven and on earth and under the earth, and every tongue will confess that Jesus Christ is Lord, to the glory of God the Father.[51]

God literally reached down to save us in Christ. Christ paid our penalty of death, and this same one who defeated death brought us new life. The symbol of the church throughout all the ages has been the cross. We forget what a horrible thing it really was. It is of the same equivalence as putting a picture of an electric chair on our church wall.

The message of God being crucified for us has been seen from many people's perspectives as a joke. On an inscription found in the Palatine, the imperial residential district in Rome, under what is believed to be the oldest crucifix in existence (probably from around the third century), we find this sarcastic scribble: "Alexmenos worships his God." Above these words is a picture of a crucified man with a donkey's head.[52] Paul knew what he was talking about when he wrote *"So when we preach that Christ was crucified, the Jews are offended, and the Gentiles say it's all nonsense."*[53]

About the cross Goethe wrote:

---

[51] Phil. 2:5-11.

[52] Hans Kung, *On Being A Christian* (Great Britain, Glasgow: Fount, 1978) p. 396.

[53] 1 Cor. 1:23.

A lightweight little ceremonial cross always adds to life's [happiness]; no reasonable [person] should bother to dig up and replant the dismal cross of Calvary, the most repulsive thing under the sun.[54]

Even D. T. Suzuki, the prominent Zen Buddhist, said, "When I see a crucified figure of Christ I cannot help thinking of the gap that lies deep between Christianity and Buddhism."[55]

God humiliated himself so that we could be glorified. Because God, through Christ, suffered and died on our behalf and defeated sin and death on our behalf, he has the right to say, "I'm number one. Worship no one but me."

Hans Kung sums this up nicely: "The resurrection message...reveals the very thing that was not to be expected: that this crucified Jesus, despite everything, *was right*."[56]

Conclusion

The first commandment states *"I am the LORD your God, who rescued you from slavery in Egypt. Do not worship any other gods besides me."*[37] God gave us this commandment as the first of all his commandments so that we would put things in their proper place. Wisdom is found when we surrender to the God revealed to us in the Bible.[57] He is number one simply because it is true to reality, because he himself is the only one who ever fully and completely

---

[54] Hans Kung, *On Being A Christian* (Great Britain, Glasgow: Fount, 1978) p. 397.

[55] Ibid.

[56] Ibid., p. 382.

[57] Prov. 1:7.

saved humanity, and because he, through Christ, suffered, died, and defeated sin and death on our behalf.

Wayne Gretzky, the Beatles, Bill Gates, America, Canada, and even you and I will fade like the grass, but the God who has revealed himself in the Bible was, is, and always will be number one.[58]

---

[58] Rev. 1:8.

CHAPTER THREE

Put Away Your Idols

Do not make idols of any kind, whether in the shape of birds or animals or fish. You must never worship or bow down to them, for I, the LORD your God, am a jealous God who will not share your affection with any other god![59]

When I was in grade one, I discovered gold in our backyard. I thought I was going to make my parents rich! I found a couple of ice cream buckets in the garage and filled them with this fortune that seemed to be all over our lawn. With pride I brought these pails of gold to my mother, and to my horror she rushed me to the bathroom to wash my hands. It wasn't gold I discovered; it was rabbit droppings. What I thought would change the economic status of my family forever ended up being something that made me scrub my hands for days. It didn't matter how much I believed it was gold. It didn't matter how sincere I was. I had discovered rabbit poo.

In the same way, people chase after all kinds of things that look real and promising. We can build, create, and accomplish huge dreams, even in the name of God, but they can end up having as much value as rabbit poo.

---

[59] Deut. 5:8-9.

The second commandment that God gave us states:

Do not make idols of any kind, whether in the shape of birds or animals or fish. You must never worship or bow down to them, for I, the LORD your God, am a jealous God who will not share your affection with any other god![59]

When we read this commandment against idolatry it is easy to overlook the personal application and see it as only speaking to pagan tribes that dance and bow before a carved piece of wood or stone. With our "sophisticated" intellect we silently scoff at these "uncivilized" and "uneducated" people groups. We concur with the words of Jeremiah who wrote:

Their ways are futile and foolish. They cut down a tree and carve an idol. They decorate it with gold and silver and then fasten it securely with hammer and nails so it won't fall over. There stands their god like a helpless scarecrow in a garden! It cannot speak, and it needs to be carried because it cannot walk. Do not be afraid of such gods, for they can neither harm you nor do you any good.[60]

We also agree with Isaiah who wrote:

He cuts down cedars; he selects the cypress and the oak; he plants the cedar in the forest to be nourished by the rain. And after his care, he uses part of the wood to make a fire to warm himself and bake his bread. Then—yes, it's true—he takes the rest of it and makes himself a god for people to worship! He makes an idol and bows down

---

[60] Jer. 10:3-5.

and praises it! He burns part of the tree to roast his meat and to keep himself warm. Then he takes what's left and makes his god: a carved idol! He falls down in front of it, worshiping and praying to it. "Rescue me!" he says. "You are my god!"

Such stupidity and ignorance! Their eyes are closed, and they cannot see. Their minds are shut, and they cannot think. The person who made the idol never stops to reflect, "Why, it's just a block of wood! I burned half of it for heat and used it to bake my bread and roast my meat. How can the rest of it be a god? Should I bow down to worship a chunk of wood?" The poor, deluded fool feeds on ashes. He is trusting something that can give him no help at all. Yet he cannot bring himself to ask, "Is this thing, this idol that I'm holding in my hand, a lie?"[61]

We must question whether these warnings only apply to tribal pagan worship. If we are honest, should we not admit that we also have a tendency to worship that which our own hands have created? It may not look like a Baal altar or an Asherah pole, but it may take the form of a small business, a house, a time-share, an educational pursuit, a sports team, or even a church ministry. When we search for meaning in these things, we need to realize that we are just as idolatrous as anyone else. We've exchanged old gods for new ones and simply changed their names. We cannot escape this. The philosopher Cicero recognized that "the seed of religion is planted in everyone." Nobody gets rid of their gods; they

---

[61] Isa. 44:16-20.

merely worship different ones. Everyone worships something—even the avid atheist.

The Idol of Progress

The social questions we ask each other show our tendency to idolize our creations. We more frequently ask what another person *does* than who the other person *is*. We want to find out what's been achieved, what a person's position or social standing is, and whether or not they contribute or are a burden on society. We are told to stay away from discussing religious and political issues because those are personal—too close to the heart of who a person is. It is what people *do* that we want to know, for that is what we tend to worship. Words like *work, career, money, industrializing, producing, expanding, consuming, growth, progress, perfection, improvement,* and *goals* are the vocabulary of this idolatrous religion.

The Idol of the Fast-Paced Life

The speed at which we live our life is another modern idol. This is also one of the factors in our being able to merely poke around in different spiritualities without really understanding them. We look for quick answers, instant healings, and immediate escape from the troubles of life. This loss of time to think, reflect, study, play, and worship (in other words, to do truly human things) makes us less than human. The fact that we brag about how busy we are and the fact that workaholism has become a socially acceptable disease should warn us that the pace of our lives has become another one of our idols. As Erwin Lutzer points out: "[From the perspective of many Christians] smoking is condemned because our body is the temple of the Holy Spirit, but one who lives on insufficient sleep is considered diligent."[62]

In the pantheon of modern gods, the goddess "Fast-Paced Life" is married to the god "Success."

The Idol of Religion

Another idolatry, one that Christians can easily fall into, is the worship of worship or the worship of spiritual experience. Whenever we've been practising something in a certain way for a long period of time we have the danger of seeing the form as just as sacred as the One the form should be pointing to. Jesus was addressing this when he said, *"You ignore God's specific laws and substitute your own traditions."*[63] For example, the Catholic church has been in danger of worshipping the mass. The Orthodox churches have been in danger of worshipping the statues and pictures they erect. The Pentecostals have been in danger of worshipping certain spiritual gifts. The Anglicans have been in danger of worshipping their liturgy. The Baptists have been in danger of worshipping their form of church government. One of the great dangers today, for many Christians across denominational lines, is the worship of a certain style of music. When we begin to place more importance on these issues and the feelings they give us than on our call to discipleship, holiness, and love for God and one another, we are then serving idols rather than the true God. Don't misinterpret what I am saying; communion, pictures, spiritual gifts, liturgy, church government, baptism, and music are all good things when they point beyond themselves to the

[62] Erwin Lutzer, *How in the World can I be Holy?* (Chicago, IL: Moody, 1974) p. 91.

[63] Mark 7:8.

Alpha and the Omega. It is when they become idols that we are breaking the second commandment.

The Idols of Good Luck Charms, Superstition, and Celebrities

Idolatry can also show up in the form of a good luck charm. This can be seen when we absolutely have to have something with us, on us, or by us before we can do something else. I've talked to some Christians who have a hard time playing a sporting event if a certain gold cross isn't around their neck or they aren't wearing their WWJD bracelet around their wrist. These can be great reminders of our commitment to Christ, but again, if they become the focus of our attention they have become an idol.

What about superstition? Does it make sense to be a Christian and then be afraid if a black cat walks across your path or you break a mirror? What about your burial? I've had Christians tell me they are afraid they will lose their salvation if they are cremated. Is that in the gospel? Does the resurrection actually lose its power because of the method by which your body is decomposed? After I explained this to one person, they told me that they still wouldn't be cremated *just in case.* That's still idolatry. Faith in God is trust without the superstitious *just in case.* So go ahead, break those mirrors, and walk without fear.

Celebrities can be another idol. Many Christians have their Christian celebrities. They will drive for days just to hear a certain band, and they get into such an emotional frenzy that they are willing to respond to anything the band says. Christian preachers can also be held up to an almost cult-figure status. Some Christians will believe anything their favourite preacher says or their favourite author writes and are hardly able to listen to anyone else without comparing them to their super-disciple. For example, Billy Graham is a wonderful man of God, but try making even the slightest criticism about him and his ministry and some people will question your salvation. Billy Graham is not God! He, and his evangelistic methods, are not above loving evaluation, accountability, and possible rebuke at times. I'm sure Dr. Graham would be the first to agree with this. No preacher or church leader is the final authority. As a church we should respect and honour our leaders, but we should never make them into idols.

Learning to Put Things in their Proper Place: The Other Side—The Arts

Many evangelical churches have shied away from the arts because of the abuse attributed to them at different times throughout church history. For instance, during the Reformation a number of evangelically minded church leaders, like Carlstadt, the famous colleague of Martin Luther, encouraged the physical destruction of church icons and stained glass windows.[64] Carlstadt's followers put rocks through the windows of these churches and destroyed many precious pieces of art. This was not the best way to make his point, and it was the start of much evangelical dissociation from the arts. Instead, these churches are usually

---

[64] Martin Luther did not agree with Carlstadt's approach on this issue.

noted for their very basic church buildings, with a cross, a pulpit, and an open Bible as their only symbols (some don't even have those). Some evangelicals even argue that the arts are simply a waste of money. This loss of the arts has been a great detriment for these churches, making them voiceless within the artistic and cultural communities. Sure, as we said regarding all the other issues mentioned in this chapter, the arts can become idols, but they don't have to.

The second commandment does not suggest that Christians should stay out of the arts any more than it says Christians should not wear crosses, worship, sing in church, read books or listen to preachers. This commandment is simply telling us that we are to put God first and make sure everything else is in its proper place.

When the Idols Take Over

The false gods and idols we create eventually turn on us and bind us—like in those bad science fiction movies, where the very creatures that the humans create turn on their creators. The idols we build become our Frankensteins. They really do end up controlling us and becoming our gods. If we wrap our lives around our businesses, our homes, our governments, our successes, our superstitions, our favorite styles of music, our celebrities, or our particular denominations, these things can and will turn on us, disappoint us, and possibly destroy our lives. One theologian said it in these words:

> True freedom means that people are liberated from dependence on and obligations to the false gods who drive them on mercilessly to new achievements:

money or career, prestige or power, or whatever is the supreme value for them.[65]

What the Second Command is Teaching us

Do not make idols of any kind, whether in the shape of birds or animals or fish. You must never worship or bow down to them, for I, the LORD your God, am a jealous God who will not share your affection with any other god![59]

Let us not worship what we do, what we create, what we build, or what we are comfortable with, but let us use these things to glorify God and to point others to him. Let us also not worship our worship or have good luck charms, superstitions, and blind allegiance to celebrities, but in all things let us glorify God and show others that we do truly believe that he is number one.

I, the LORD your God, am a jealous God who will not share your affection with any other god! I do not leave unpunished the sins of those who hate me, but I punish the children for the sins of their parents to the third and fourth generations. But I lavish my love on those who love me and obey my commands, even for a thousand generations.[66]

God is a jealous God, and, as we saw in the last chapter, he has the right to be so and he has the right to expect our full allegiance. Unlike the idols we build, which turn us into their slaves, the God of the Bible calls us to surrender

---

[65] Hans Kung, *On Being a Christian* (Great Britain: Collins, 1974) p. 589.

[66] Deut. 5:9-10.

to him and, when we do, he gives us freedom. Paul writes these words to the followers of the God of the Bible:

> *Sin is no longer your master, for you are no longer subject to the law, which enslaves you to sin. Instead, you are free by God's grace.*
>
> *So since God's grace has set us free from the law, does this mean we can go on sinning? Of course not! Don't you realize that whatever you choose to obey becomes your master? You can choose sin, which leads to death, or you can choose to obey God and receive his approval. Thank God! Once you were slaves of sin, but now you have obeyed with all your heart the new teaching God has given you. Now you are free from sin, your old master, and you have become slaves to your new master, righteousness.*[67]

What a great truth! When we think we are free to live for ourselves, we find out we are actually slaves to sin and idolatry, and when we give our lives over to Christ and become his slave, we find ourselves truly free.

Why should we live for the idols we create? They have no way of listening to us, comforting us, guiding us, or knowing us personally. In fact, they do the opposite. They slowly take over our lives, like a drug that we end up helplessly serving. Nothing in life can satisfy us except the true God. He is a good God! Only through him can we find satisfaction, meaning, purpose, and value. That is God's promise. When we take God out of his proper place, we simply gather rabbit droppings—fool's gold, with ourselves as the fool![68]

---

[67] Rom. 6:14-18.

[68] Jer. 2:23-37.

So, my dear friends, flee from the worship of idols. You are reasonable people. Decide for yourselves if what I am about to say is true.... Whatever you eat or drink or whatever you do, you must do all for the glory of God.[69]

---

[69] 1 Cor. 10:14-15, 31.

CHAPTER FOUR
In God's Name

Do not misuse the name of the LORD your God.
The LORD will not let you go unpunished
if you misuse his name.[70]

A clergyman of the Anglican church stood behind the pulpit poised to preach. When it seemed that no sound was coming through the speakers, he tapped the microphone and muttered under his breath, "Oh Lord, something's wrong with you." But the microphone was working. The congregation heard his words, and, having expected to hear "The Lord be with you," they all responded in unison, "And also with you."

The third commandment reads: *"Do not misuse the name of the LORD your God. The LORD will not let you go unpunished if you misuse his name."*[70]

What does it mean to *misuse* the name of the Lord? The most common idea is that this commandment is speaking against swearing. We are going to find out in this chapter, however, that it refers to a lot more than swearing.

---

[70] Deut. 5:11.

43

1. Swearing or Cursing

Let's begin with the issue of swearing, however, since it is *one* of the ways that the Lord's name can be misused. All you have to do is visit a local high school or some work environments to find out how popular the name of Jesus Christ is. When we use God's name in this way, it is a very serious sin. In fact, it is blasphemy.

In the Bible, names were important. The character and personality of an individual was often described by the name they were given. For example, the name *Abraham* meant "father of many nations," *Israel* meant "wrestler with God," and *Jesus* meant "Saviour." In many instances, the names of individuals were changed after a significant event in their life. We find this to be the case with *Abram* being changed to *Abraham*, *Sarai* to *Sarah*, *Jacob* to *Israel*, *Simon* to *Peter*, and *Saul* to *Paul*. In the early days of the church, it was a common practice for those coming out of a pagan culture and converting to Christianity to change their name to represent their change of allegiance. It is from this tradition that we hear of people receiving a "Christian" name. In many of our circles this is not practiced any more. However, the principle of having a "good" name is still important. As the Bible teaches:

> *Choose a good reputation over great riches, for being held in high esteem is better than having silver or gold.*[71]
>
> *A good reputation is more valuable than the most expensive perfume.*[72]

---

[71] Prov. 22:1.
[72] Eccl. 7:1.

What does all this have to do with swearing and misusing the Lord's name? A lot! Just as names in the Bible were closely connected to a person's character, so the names for God teach us about his character. There are many names for God in the Bible. Some of the more popular ones are *Yahweh*, which means "I am who I am," *Elohim*, which means "Majesty," *Adonai*, which means "Lord," *Rahum*, which means "Merciful," and *Elyon*, which means "Most High." Jesus referred to God as *Abba*, which means "Father," and Christians throughout history have described the God of the Bible as the *Trinity*, which means "one God in three persons."

To use the name of God as a swear word is to associate him with things that are contrary to his nature. That is why it is blasphemy. When we curse in God's name we smear his name by connecting it with something against his character. It is the same as spreading lies or gossiping about another person. God's holiness is to be protected, not for his sake but for ours. That is why God threatens that he *"will not let you go unpunished if you misuse his name."* There will be consequences. The holy, righteous, honourable name of God should not be used as a swear word.

2. Flippancy

Another way we can misuse the name of God is to use it flippantly. Often this is not meant to be vindictive, and so it comes across as innocent. Many Christians fall into this trap. It manifests itself in those little phrases "oh god," or "oh my god," or sometimes just "god!"[73]

This is wrong because it reduces the name of God, and

---

[73] I refuse to capitalize *god* in this instance.

that which represents his personhood, to meaninglessness. It is hard to convince someone that God is the All-Powerful One, worthy of our worship, when they continually hear phrases like "oh my god," "oh god," and "god, no" from the one trying to convince them. In one breath, *god* is a meaningless expression of speech thrown around for every little trivial thing that comes across our path, and with the other breath we try to tell our friends that he is the Saviour and Life-Giver of humanity to whom we all must one day surrender.

When we use God's name in this kind of flippant and meaningless way, we empty it of content and make it irrelevant. Phrases like "oh rats" or "fiddlesticks" are fine, because they *are* meaningless and do not have any content, authority, or honour associated with them. "Oh rats," however, should never be in the same category as "oh my god." Unlike "fiddlesticks," we pray in the name of Jesus. The name of Christ causes demons to submit,[74] the dead to rise,[75] broken hearts to be mended,[76] the sick to be healed,[77] the blind to be given sight,[78] sinners to receive forgiveness,[79] and salvation to be found.[80] Never should we take a name like this and reduce it to a phrase like "oh my god, that guy is cute." That, too, is blaspheming!

[74] Luke 4:40-41; 8:26-39; 10:17.
[75] Luke 8:49-56, John 11.
[76] John 4.
[77] Luke 8:40-48.
[78] Luke 18:35-43.
[79] Luke 7:36-50.
[80] John 3:16-17; 14:6.

3. Oaths

A third way to misuse the name of God is to use it as a bargaining tool to try and give more weight to something you are saying. This shows up when we say things like: "I swear on the Bible that I am telling you the truth."[81] "As God is my witness, I did not do it." "Lord, I promise you, if you just get me out of this mess, I'll start reading my Bible every day." "Lord, if I win the lottery, I'll give half of my money to the poor—I promise."

A number of individuals throughout church history ended up in monasteries because of rash vows. One of these cases happened on a July afternoon in 1505. A twenty-one-year-old man named Martin Luther was walking back to Erfurt (in Germany) after a ten-day visit with his parents. Suddenly a dark, violent storm broke out and lightning struck a nearby tree, which split in two before his eyes. Fearing for his life, young Martin Luther fell to the ground and cried out, "Saint Anne! Save me! If you spare me, I promise I will become a monk!" Martin Luther did not die in that storm, and off to the monastery he went. The rest is history!

The Gospel writer Matthew records these words of Jesus:

> *"Again, you have heard that the law of Moses says, 'Do not break your vows; you must carry out the vows you have made to the LORD.' But I say, don't make any vows! If you say, 'By heaven!' it is a sacred vow because*

---

[81] I do not believe that this means we should never "swear" on the Bible in a court of law if we are asked to—provided we tell the truth. Some Christians, however, have felt that doing this is wrong.

heaven is God's throne. And if you say, 'By the earth!' it is a sacred vow because the earth is his footstool. And don't swear, 'By Jerusalem!' for Jerusalem is the city of the great King. Don't even swear, 'By my head!' for you can't turn one hair white or black. Just say a simple, 'Yes, I will,' or 'No, I won't.' Your word is enough. To strengthen your promise with a vow shows that something is wrong." [82]

Why does Jesus tell us to keep away from oaths? Why does he warn us against calling on the name of God in an attempt to give extra merit to what we are saying? The reason Jesus does this is because he wants us to be the kind of people who have enough integrity, and a good enough name, that people will simply take us at our word. An extra "I swear on the Bible" only breeds suspicion. Is our word not good enough? Why the need for extra authority?

God is not into bargaining. To make a promise like "God, if you do this then I'll do that" is called business, not worship. God doesn't want us becoming missionaries or witnessing in an attempt to rack up brownie points. God wants us to serve him because we love him and have a desire to worship him.

A few years back I coached an under-fourteen boys' soccer team. I enjoyed it when the guys played hard simply because they wanted to make me proud, but it got under my skin when they tried to get something out of me for their performance. The first time one of my players said "Coach, if you'll buy me a Coke after tonight's game I promise to play hard" was the first time I made a player

---

[82] Matt. 5:33-37.

sit and watch the rest of his team play. If it wasn't for the parents standing around I would probably have sent him home or made him sit the entire game. I can't stand that kind of attitude—"I'll do it for you if I get something out of it"—and neither can God.

Jesus taught us the same thing regarding vows. He has called us to get in the game of life and play for God's side. He doesn't want us living for him only *if* he does this, that, or some other thing for us. God is not a genie. We should not misuse his name with empty promises and vows.

Many Christians have tried to play the bargaining game of oaths with God. When we do so, we misuse his name. When our surrender to God includes "As soon as the kids leave the home," "As soon as I'm married," "Lord, once I make a bit more money," "As soon as I'm healthy," "Once we're settled in," "As soon as I am better grounded in my faith," "As soon as I finish my education," "Once I'm overseas," "As soon as I discover my spiritual gift," "As soon as someone asks," or "Once I find a good church," we misuse his name. Instead, Jesus said, *"Anyone who puts a hand to the plow and then looks back is not fit for the Kingdom of God."*[83]

Don't misuse the name of the Lord. Jesus warned us not to attach his name to our laundry list of life's ifs, ands, and buts. Instead, he told us to *"just say a simple, 'Yes, I will,' or 'No, I won't.' Your word is enough. To strengthen your promise with a vow shows that something is wrong."*[84]

The name of God is not a wild card to be played in times of trouble. Instead, before this God *"every knee will*

---

[83] Luke 9:62.

[84] Matt. 5:37.

bow to me and every tongue will confess allegiance.[85]

"Do not misuse the name of the LORD *your God. The* LORD *will not let you go unpunished if you misuse his name."*[86]

Conclusion

God's name is not to be used as a curse or a swear word, for when we do that we take something holy and smear it with something ugly. God's name is not to be used in a flippant way, for when we do that we take something powerful and reduce it to something meaningless. God's name is not to be used in making rash oaths or promises, for when we do that we turn the throne of God into a bargaining table.

We would all do well to remember the warning given to us by James: *"If you claim to be religious but don't control your tongue, you are just fooling yourself, and your religion is worthless."*[87]

May we honour God in the way we revere and treat his name!

---

[85] Rom. 14:11.
[86] Deut. 5:11.
[87] Jas. 1:26.

CHAPTER FIVE
Rest and Relaxation

Observe the Sabbath day by keeping it holy, as the LORD your God has commanded you. Six days a week are set apart for your daily duties and regular work, but the seventh day is a day of rest dedicated to the LORD your God. On that day no one in your household may do any kind of work. This includes you, your sons and daughters, your male and female servants, your oxen and donkeys and other livestock, and any foreigners living among you. All your male and female servants must rest as you do.
Remember that you were once slaves in Egypt and that the LORD your God brought you out with amazing power and mighty deeds. That is why the LORD your God has commanded you to observe the Sabbath day.[88]

When we think of a traditional week of work we think of Monday through Friday, forty hours a week, with the weekends off. As society continues to get increasingly complex, however, this traditional way of working is becoming less common. Today we are increasingly on call, working evening shifts, job sharing, working two or some-times three jobs, and keeping stores open twenty-four hours a day, seven days a week. As a college student I spent my summers delivering pizza from 5:00 p.m. to 2:00 a.m. on weekends and from 5:00 p.m. to 12:00 a.m. on weeknights. Because I didn't want to get bored, and because I inherited my father's work ethic, I also drove a Zamboni for the local arena in the mornings and volun-

---

[88] Deut. 5:12-15.

teered at different kids' camps for a local church in the afternoons. As a pastor of a church now, I don't know if I've ever experienced "nine to five."[89]

Henri Nouwen wrote:

Modern (people) do not just eat and drink, but have business lunches and fund-raising dinners. [They] do not just go horse-back riding or swimming—[they invite] their companions to do a little business on horse-back or even in the pool...A life like this cannot be celebrated because we are constantly concerned with changing it into something else, always trying to do something to it, get something out of it, and make it fit into our plans and projects. We go to meetings, conferences, and congresses. We critically evaluate our part, discuss how to do it better in the future, and worry whether or not our great design will ever work out.[90]

In the midst of this, the fourth commandment speaks out:

Observe the Sabbath day by keeping it holy, as the LORD your God has commanded you. Six days a week are set apart for your daily duties and regular work, but the seventh day is a day of rest dedicated to the LORD your God. On that day no one in your household may do any kind of work. This includes you, your sons and daughters, your male and female servants, your oxen and donkeys and other livestock, and any foreigners living among

---

[89] Some people feel very differently about the work of the clergy. One congregation complained that their pastor was "invisible six days a week and incomprehensible on the seventh."

[90] Henri Nouwen, *Creative Ministry* (USA: Image, 1978) pp. 101-102.

you. All your male and female servants must rest as you do. Remember that you were once slaves in Egypt and that the LORD your God brought you out with amazing power and mighty deeds. That is why the LORD your God has commanded you to observe the Sabbath day.[88]

To Rest is Divine—To Rest is to be Human!

The ability to quit doing and simply be is divine. Like all of God's commandments this one comes out of who God is. In Genesis we read:

On the seventh day, having finished his task, God rested from all his work. And God blessed the seventh day and declared it holy, because it was the day when he rested from his work of creation.[91]

This verse does not mean that God rested because he grew tired. We know this from God's words recorded in the book of Isaiah:

Have you never heard or understood? Don't you know that the LORD is the everlasting God, the Creator of all the earth? He never grows faint or weary. No one can measure the depths of his understanding.[92]

Why, then, did God rest on the seventh day? He rested to show us that he is complete in himself. Work is not what makes God who he is. God's self-worth is not determined by what he produces. He is complete in rest. As fallen humans we often make the mistake of looking for approval and identity in our work. The sin of workaholism has

[91] Gen. 2:2-3.
[92] Isa. 40:28.

become socially acceptable. It even gives us certain bragging rights and esteem in the eyes of others. Rest, however, does not threaten God! In fact, it shows him to be the God *over* work, not a God driven by work.[93]

God does not need to work or to rest, yet he worked and then rested on the seventh day as a model for humanity. The Sabbath day was established for *us*. Jesus reminded us of this when he said, *"The Sabbath was made to benefit people, and not people to benefit the Sabbath."*[94] Then, alluding to his divinity, Jesus reminds us that God doesn't need the Sabbath but is the Lord over the Sabbath. *"And I, the Son of Man, am master even of the Sabbath!"*[95]

In God's goodness he created a Sabbath rest for the pleasure of men and women. He established the Sabbath as a reminder to humanity that their worth is not found in their work but in who they are. In fact, to work and never play is to be *less* than human. To not rest is to be a machine. God truly did give us these commands for our own protection and pleasure. He gave them to us to protect our humanity. A human being is not someone controlled by work. To be human is to be able to stop, rest, rejoice, dance, laugh, think and reflect. Henri Nouwen wrote: "Our culture is a working, hurrying, and worrying culture with many opportunities except the opportunity to celebrate life."[96]

---

[93] If God needed work to be God, he would be dependent upon work for his being. This would make work, and not God, the ultimate power. Work submits to God. Work happens when God says so, and work stops when God says so.

[94] Mark 2:27.

[95] Mark, 2:28.

[96] Henri Nouwen, *Creative Ministry* (USA: Image, 1978) p. 101-102.

After God created, he rejoiced at what he had made and proclaimed it "very good!"[97] God then celebrated and enjoyed his creation. He took delight in what he had done. God rested!

Alice's Nonsense

A few summers ago, my wife and I travelled to England and stopped for a day at Oxford. There we visited the house that Lewis Carroll once lived in. Inspired by the atmosphere, I decided to read his *Alice's Adventures in Wonderland* and *Through the Looking Glass*. Talk about a frustrating experience! I struggled in vain to discover the plot. I couldn't understand where anything was going. The stories didn't solve any problems or reach any logical conclusions but seemed to consist of random, pointless events.[98] I wanted to *get* something out of those stories. I wanted to find something in them that I could *use*.[99] I grew angry with Carroll for wasting my time. I did force my way through them so that I could at least feel like I had accomplished something.

Then, at the end of *Alice's Adventures in Wonderland*, I found an interesting letter by Lewis Carroll in which he explains that the books were supposed to be nonsense. They were written from the mind of a child at play. Things were not supposed to *go* anywhere. The tales were not supposed to *do* anything. It was play, fun, rest, and nonsense—and I found it annoying! In that letter Carroll wrote:

---

[97] Gen. 1:31.

[98] My apologies to those English buffs who delight in finding all kinds of hidden and symbolic innuendos in the subconscious of the author.

[99] Ironically, I did find something in them to use, as I am using them right now.

I do not believe that God means [for us] to divide life into two halves—to wear a grave face on Sunday, and to think it out-of-place to even so much as mention him on a weekday. Do you think he only comes to see kneeling figures, and to hear only tones of prayers— and that he does not also love to see the lambs leaping in the sunlight, and to hear the merry voices of the children [at play]? Surely their innocent laughter is as sweet in his ears as the greatest anthem that ever [came from] some solemn cathedral.[100]

Now I keep pictures of some of the characters from these books hanging in my office. They remind me that God has called me to worship him in rest and play.

Learning from the Children

Leaping lambs and the innocent laughter of children are sweet sounds to God, *even if they do not produce anything.* Adults and children were created not only to work[101] but to enjoy the Sabbath.[102] We are reminded of this in the Jewish Talmud, which has a wonderful line that reads: "Everyone must render an account before God of all the good things they beheld in life and did not enjoy" (Kiddushin 4:12).

Let's be honest, this makes us Protestant capitalistic products of the Industrial Revolution a little uncomfortable. Besides work and school, we want to make sure our

---

100 Lewis Carroll, *Alice's Adventures in Wonderland*, p. 151. (Unfortunately, I bought this book in England and have given it away since. I cannot remember which publication of the book this letter was found in.)

101 Gen. 2:15.

102 Deut. 5:12-15.

children don't miss out on swimming, soccer, baseball, tutoring, vacation Bible school, violin, piano, figure skating, ballet, drama, painting, and reading clubs. We wouldn't want them to get bored! The funny thing is that kids are bored more than ever today. In my experience doing lunch-hour supervision at an elementary school, I've found many kids afraid of recess. Unless something is *organized* for them, what is there to do? Are our children losing their ability to have an imagination like Alice's? This is a direct violation of the forth commandment. Children's humour has become more sarcastic and "adult" rather than innocent and fun. Many people have acknowledged that "children are growing up too fast these days." Is this because too many adults have forgotten how to be childlike? Didn't Jesus warn us about this?

> *Jesus called a small child over to him and put the child among them. Then he said, "I assure you, unless you turn from your sins and become as little children, you will never get into the kingdom of heaven."*[103]

"If you want to enjoy me," Jesus says, "if you want to turn from your sin, from breaking the fourth commandment, and enter into the Sabbath, you must become like a little child."

The fourth commandment teaches us:

> *Observe the Sabbath day by keeping it holy, as the LORD your God has commanded you. Six days a week are set apart for your daily duties and regular work, but the seventh day is a day of rest dedicated to the LORD your God.*

---

[103] Matt. 18:2-3.

On that day no one in your household may do any kind
of work. This includes you, your sons and daughters,
your male and female servants, your oxen and donkeys
and other livestock, and any foreigners living among
you. All your male and female servants must rest as you
do. Remember that you were once slaves in Egypt and
that the LORD your God brought you out with amazing
power and mighty deeds. That is why the LORD your God
has commanded you to observe the Sabbath day.[88]

What About Going to Church?

At this point you may be thinking, "All this talk
about keeping the Sabbath day *holy* and we haven't even
mentioned going to church." This is because Sabbath
keeping and going to church have nothing to do with
each other! Now, before you charge me with heresy, keep
reading.[104] The Bible clearly teaches us that regular
involvement in a biblical church is essential for spiritual
growth,[105] but that is a separate issue from Sabbath.
There is nothing wrong with having the day you attend
church be your day of Sabbath, but it does not have to be
that way.[106] Working on Sunday, worshipping with your

---

[104] Also, you will see in chapter 8 of my book *All Roads Lead
Somewhere* how essential it is for a Christian to be a part of a local
church and not forsake meeting with a community of believers.

[105] Heb. 10:23-25 (see Acts 2:41-42 on the core characteristics of
a biblical church).

[106] This cannot be used as an excuse for not helping out at your
local church. If you choose to keep Sunday as your complete day of
rest, there are still six other days in the week that your church could
use you. It is spiritually unhealthy to attend a church and not contribute any of your time, gifts, and money.

church community at a Thursday night service, and taking Saturdays as your Sabbath would be a totally biblical, healthy way to live. We must make sure we are obeying the principle of this command in a biblical manner and not simply through the eyes of human tradition. Jesus constantly challenged the religious establishment's wrong understanding of Sabbath.[107] Paul also warns about legalism regarding the Sabbath:

> Don't let anyone condemn you for what you eat or drink, or for not celebrating certain holy days or new-moon ceremonies or Sabbaths. For these rules were only shadows of the real thing, Christ himself.[108]

Instead of understanding this God-given freedom and the fact that God gave us the Sabbath for our protection and pleasure, many in the church struggle with repressive human laws that they have been taught regarding the Sabbath. Listen to these totally unbiblical words regarding the Sabbath, expressed by the Puritans in the "Great Westminster Divines' Meeting and Assembly":

> "The Lord's day ought to be so remembered...to which end...there [is to be] holy resting all day from all unnecessary labors; and an abstaining, not only from all sports and pastimes, but also from all worldly words and thoughts...What time is vacant, between or after the solemn meeting of the congregation in public, [should] be spent in reading, meditation, recitation of sermons, [family devotions], holy conferences, prayers, singing, visiting the sick,

---

[107] Matt. 12:1-14; Mark 2:23-28; Luke 6:1-11; John 9.
[108] Col. 2:16-17.

relieving the poor and other like duties of piety, charity, and mercy."[109]

That Puritan day of rest makes me tired just thinking about it! Jonathan Edwards, the great American theologian and preacher of the eighteenth century, dealt with the cultural issue of what can and cannot be done on the Sabbath as well. As one writer puts it:

> [Jonathan Edwards and his wife Sarah were evidently] intimate on the Lord's Day. Colonial New Englanders believed that babies were born on the same day of the week as conceived. When six of the Edwards' 11 children arrived on Sundays, it sent tongues wagging. Such intimacy wasn't appropriate Sunday behaviour.[110]

These kinds of legalistic Sabbath-keeping laws caused the cultural satirist Mark Twain to write to one of his Christian friends:

> You will never know, never divine, guess, imagine, how loathsome a thing the Christian religion can be made until you come to know and study [my Christian friend] Cable daily and hourly...He has taught me to abhor and detest the Sabbath-day and hunt up new and troublesome ways to dishonor it.[111]

---

[109] Stuart Briscoe, *The Ten Commandments* (Wheaton, IL: Harold Shaw, 1986) pp. 62-63.

[110] Robert J. Morgan, *On This Day* (Nashville, TN: Thomas Nelson, 1997) July 28.

[111] Andrew, Hoffman, *Inventing Mark Twain* (New York, NY: Quill, 1997) p. 321.

Now, don't get me wrong. Many of the things documented in that Puritan Westminster Divines' Meeting are good, but let's spread them over the week and make them a lifestyle. The danger of the legalism in this Puritan statement and in cultural rules like the one that Jonathan Edwards faced, like all legalism, is the religious façade it creates. Why should we abstain from worldly words and thoughts *on the Lord's Day*? Shouldn't we strive to do that all the time? Isn't it this kind of thinking that produces "Sunday Christians"? In regards to the Jonathan Edwards situation, why is sex seen as a secular act of work and not a holy one of enjoyment and rest? Does that not just perpetuate the myth that sex is really dirty and not something that God is very pleased about?[112]

The biblical commandment about Sabbath is about rest, not about abstaining from secular duties so as to engage in religious ones. The Sabbath is holy precisely because *rest is holy*. Taking a day off to celebrate life, to play football with your kids, to go for a walk or a bike ride, to bird watch, to have a barbecue with your neighbours, or to just read a novel, is keeping the Sabbath. These are holy, worshipful acts!

Learning from Past Mistakes

Some of the great saints of the Evangelical tradition did many wonderful things yet never figured out Sabbath. In some instances we have idolized what these men did because we have devalued Sabbath. This is not to take away from their many great accomplishments or to acknowledge

---

[112] See commandment seven for a further discussion on this topic.

the fact that God still works despite imperfections, yet we would be wise to not repeat their mistakes. I could give numerous examples, but allow me to pick on the eighteenth century preachers John Wesley and George Whitefield.

John Wesley, the man behind the Methodist movement, regularly preached two or three times a day for weeks on end. After his usual two-hour sermons were over, he would spend many more hours praying for and counselling others, as well as spending time daily in prayer and study. In order not to waste any time, he wrote many of his sermons and devoured many books while travelling from town to town on horseback. In addition to this already unbelievable agenda, he wrote over 200 books during his lifetime. Wow! That's incredible! At the same time, however, his wife divorced him. She probably got tired of seeing his backside going out the front door. Despite all the good that Wesley did, he never learned the meaning of Sabbath.

George Whitefield began his ministry by praying, "God, may I not have a wife till I can live as though I had none." Though he should have taken Paul's advice and not married, he unfortunately did. During their week-long honeymoon, Whitefield preached twice a day in the surrounding countryside.[113] He crossed the Atlantic thirteen times during his ministry and was once gone for over two years.[114] Even when Whitefield's four-month-old son died, he did not stop his preaching ministry. In fact, he was preaching a sermon out in a nearby field when he heard the

---

[113] Further evidence that he should have stayed single, as he must have had the gift of celibacy.

[114] See what I mean about that gift of celibacy?

bells from his own son's funeral ringing in the distance. Between 1736 and 1770, this travelling evangelist preached more than eighteen thousand times to crowds of thousands in Great Britain, Northern Europe, and the American colonies. Because of this, he spent many days sick, bedridden and coughing up blood. He eventually died from physical exhaustion on September 30, 1770, at the age of fifty-five. Although there are many amazing things about this man's life, there is also much that is pathetic. George Whitefield never learned how to keep Sabbath.

I could go on and tell you similar stories of men like Hudson Taylor, who said, "Rest? There is too much to do. I've got all of eternity to rest. God put me here to work!"[115] As noble as this may sound, it is not biblical!

Learning from the Divine-Human One

In the midst of a great storm, with waves crashing all around, while the disciples were fearing for their lives, worrying, bailing, and panicking, Jesus slept in a boat. We read:

Jesus was sleeping at the back of the boat with his head on a cushion. Frantically they woke him up, shouting, "Teacher, don't you even care that we are going to drown?"

When he woke up, he rebuked the wind and said to the water, "Quiet down!" Suddenly the wind stopped, and there was a great calm. And he asked them, "Why are you so afraid? Do you still not have faith in me?"[116]

---

[115] I have been unable to relocate where I found this quote and would appreciate being contacted with the information by anyone who does know.

[116] Mark 4:38-41.

In the gospel of Luke we find the account of Martha running around doing millions of things while her sister Mary sat at Jesus' feet and listened to him teach. As Martha's anger boiled over into a verbal rebuke of Mary's laziness, Jesus replied, *"My dear Martha, you are so upset over all these details! There is really only one thing worth being concerned about. Mary has discovered it—and I won't take it away from her."*[117]

Instead of just hating this verse, as many busy Christians have told me they do, maybe we should learn from it. We should *do* something about it. What should we do? We should *do nothing*! We should rest and learn to be "unproductive" for God.

> *So there is a special rest still waiting for the people of God. For all who enter into God's rest will find rest from their labors, just as God rested after creating the world. Let us do our best to enter that place of rest. For anyone who disobeys God, as the people of Israel did, will fall.*[118]

> *Observe the Sabbath day by keeping it holy, as the LORD your God has commanded you.*[119]

Maybe you should put this book down now and go take a nap. What a way to worship!

---

[117] Luke 11:41-42.

[118] Heb. 4:9-11.

[119] Deut. 5:12.

CHAPTER SIX
Honour Your Parents

Honor your father and mother,
as the LORD your God commanded you.
Then you will live a long, full life in the land
the LORD your God will give you.[120]

There are a number of certainties in life: we're all going to die, we're all going to pay taxes, and we all have parents. In this day of selfishness, often resulting in broken families, however, having *good* parents is becoming increasingly rare. Many people bear the emotional scars of bad or absent parents. On the other hand, there are a lot of good, dedicated, hard working, self-sacrificing, and God-honouring parents and parent figures as well. Our families, good or bad, are the number one influence in our life. Sigmund Freud wrote:

> Our intricacies, [virtues], and perversions of love, [even] the factors which determine the choice of mate and/or the success or failure in our marriages, all these can be understood only by reference to the emotional life of the child in the vortex of the family.[121]

---

[120] Deut. 5:16.

[121] Unable to find source.

Strong families are the bedrock of society. For that reason, the fifth commandment God gave states: *Honor your father and mother, as the LORD your God commanded you. Then you will live a long, full life in the land the LORD your God will give you.*[120]

Good parents are not perfect, but they do strive to care for us, invest in us, nurse us, communicate with us, teach us how to interact with and relate to the world around us, and continually remain our biggest fans. Paul reminds children of the attitude they should take with their parents when he writes, *"You children must always obey your parents, for this is what pleases the Lord."*[122] He speaks of the unregenerate by describing them as people who are *"forever inventing new ways of sinning and are disobedient to their parents."*[123] The way we respect and treat our parents tells us a lot about the state of our heart. The Lord has *commanded* us to honour our parents, and when we do so, Paul tells us, we *please* God. Again, like all the other commandments, God tells us this for our protection and pleasure when he emphasizes that *it will go well with* those who obey this.

How do we honour our parents? What does it look like? What about those parents who have been anything but a positive, godly influence on our lives? Are we really to honour them too?

God Comes First

The first place to start obeying this commandment is to remember the first one. *"Do not worship any other gods*

---

[122] Col. 3:20.
[123] Rom. 1:30.
[124] Deut. 5:7.

besides me."[124] As children of parents, we must remember that God comes before our parents. If we put our parents ahead of God we are actually dishonouring them by making them to be more than they are and God to be less than he is. No human being can fulfill us, help us find ultimate meaning, and be there for us all the time. If we expect that of another person we will suffocate them and disappoint ourselves. The best way for us to honour our parents is to make God and his will for our life more important than them and their will for our lives. Jesus taught us this when he said:

> *"If you want to be my follower you must love me more than your own father and mother, wife and children, brothers and sisters—yes, more than your own life. Otherwise, you cannot be my disciple."*[125]

If we are going to honour our parents, we need to make our relationship with God our number one priority. Only in him can we find fulfillment, peace, and joy. Only to him can we always bring our requests and burdens and find an understanding ear.[126] That is why the book of Proverbs emphasize this correct order:

> *Fear of the LORD is the beginning of knowledge. Only fools despise wisdom and discipline. Listen, my child, to what your father teaches you. Don't neglect your mother's teaching. What you learn from them will crown you with grace and clothe you with honor.*[127]

---

[125] Luke 14:26.

[126] Heb. 4:15.

[127] Prov. 1:7-9.

The fear of the Lord is the *beginning* point. After that we can *listen* to the teaching of our parents. That is the first and most important way that we are to honour our parents. God's standards are the grid through which we obey our parents. When our parents do things or ask us to do, or not do, things that go against the will of God, we must obey God instead of our parents.[128] We still treat them with dignity, but to obey God over our parents when our parents are in conflict with the will of God *is* to honour our parents.

In the same way, those of us who are parents must put God before our children. If we want our children to honour and respect us, they must see that God is first for us. This does not mean that we will never have time for our families because we are too busy "doing the Lord's work," as the last chapter pointed out. What it does mean, however, is that our children will see that our dreams, our goals, and our decisions are intimately connected with the will of God. If our identity is wrapped up in our children and there is no point at which we simply give them to God, we will fail them. We cannot constantly nag them, make decisions for them, show them how to do things better, and never let them fail. Paul said this as well, when he wrote, *"Fathers, don't aggravate your children. If you do, they will become discouraged and quit trying."*[129] Our goal as parents is to help our children learn to depend on God and not on us. When we do this we inadvertently teach them to honour us. Parents and children put the fifth commandment into practice when they put God first. Again Jesus said, *"He will*

---

[128] Acts 5:29.
[129] Col. 3:21.

give you all you need from day to day if you live for him and make the Kingdom of God your primary concern."[130]

Our Spouse Comes Second

It may seem strange that in discussing a commandment about honouring your parents I am now going to stress that spouses need to put each other ahead of their children. The reason I do this is because, after putting God first, the way you are going to teach your children to honour you is by modelling to them respect and love for your spouse. It is hard for children to honour their father and mother if their mother continually cuts down their father or their father continually ignores their mother. When we respect each other as spouses and show love and forgiveness towards one another, we not only teach our children to do the same, but we also teach them how to appropriately treat members of the opposite sex. One writer put it like this:

> Loyalty to your marriage partner should be the supreme allegiance of your life on earth, other than your commitment to God, and should supercede your loyalty to your children. If you build your life around your children, you are building a disastrous situation for the years ahead when your children leave home and you and your partner are left behind.[131]

The greatest gift you can give your children is a healthy marriage. Unhealthy marriages teach children

---

[130] Matt. 6:33.

[131] Frank Retief, *Divorce* (Cape Town, South Africa: Struik, 1990) p. 104.

negative patterns and disrespect for authority. It truly does start in the home.

If we get the hierarchy of "God first, spouse second, and children third" out of order, we break the fifth command. I am not oblivious to the fact that there are many broken families where the "spouse second" principle cannot be applied, but the purpose of this chapter, and of God's commandments, is to present God's ideal.

When parents put their children ahead of their spouse, they teach their children to disrespect them. Child-centered families instill in their children the false concept that they are the centre of the world. This perpetuates the sin of selfishness that we all struggle with. When our children are continually shown that they are number one, we encourage their sin nature and actually make it harder for them to accept and understand the gospel. How do we give a child everything and then teach them about a God who asks them to give up everything?[132] How do we tell them that the greatest commandment is to love God and others before themselves when everything in their lives has been about them?[133] It makes for a confusing message and explains much of the weakness in North American Christianity.

Our Parents Come Before Our Friends

As long as we are dependent on our parents, their authority comes before our friends. As long as our parents feed us, clothe us, pick up after us, and/or give us a free place to live, they are the authority figure in our lives that

---

[132] Matt. 19:16-30.
[133] Mark 12:30-31.

we are, after God, to obey. Even if our parents make dumb rules, like "Don't come running to me if you cut your legs off in the lawnmower" or "Don't jump off the roof and onto the wet trampoline" or "Don't point that loaded bow and arrow at you brother," we still have to obey them. If our parents have certain rules about movies and dances, it doesn't really matter if we agree or disagree with them or whether they are right or wrong, they are to be obeyed as long as we are under their authority. Only if they do, or ask us to do, something in direct violation of God's will do we have the right to disobey and suffer the consequences. To honour our parents and God means to obey them even when we do not fully understand or agree.

The book of Proverbs has a lot of great advice for those still under their parents' authority. Here is a sample:

My child, don't ignore it when the LORD disciplines you, and don't be discouraged when he corrects you. For the LORD corrects those he loves, just as a father corrects a child in whom he delights.[134]

Children who mistreat their father or chase away their mother are a public disgrace and an embarrassment. If you stop listening to instruction, my child, you have turned your back on knowledge.[135]

Listen to your father, who gave you life, and don't despise your mother's experience when she is old. Get the truth and don't ever sell it; also get wisdom, discipline, and discernment. The father of godly children has

---

[134] Prov. 3:11-12.

[135] Prov. 19:26-27.

[136] Prov. 23:22-25.

cause for joy. What a pleasure it is to have wise children. So give your parents joy! May she who gave you birth be happy.[136]

Some people curse their father and do not thank their mother. They feel pure, but they are filthy and unwashed. They are proud beyond description and disdainful.[137]

The eye that mocks a father and despises a mother will be plucked out by ravens of the valley and eaten by vultures.[138]

Whoa! That last one is nasty!
The fifth commandment teaches us:

Honor your father and mother, as the LORD *your God commanded you. Then you will live a long, full life in the land the* LORD *your God will give you.*[139]

As parents we obey and teach this commandment when we put God first, our spouse second, and our children third. As children we obey this commandment by putting God first and our parents second (as long as we are under their authority).

Society stands or falls by the health of its families. When this command is obeyed, God promises us *"full life in the land."* Again, God gives us rules for our personal well-being and for the benefit of society as a whole.

---

[137] Prov. 30:11-13.
[138] Prov. 30:17.
[139] Duet. 5:16.

CHAPTER SEVEN
Don't Murder

Do not murder.[140]

There's a joke I heard about a Sunday school teacher trying to explain the ten commandments to his class of six-year-old students. After explaining the commandment about honouring one's father and mother, he asked, "Is there a commandment that teaches us how to treat our brothers and sisters?"

Without missing a beat, one little boy spoke up. "Thou shall not murder!"

As funny as that little boy's answer was, in actuality, he showed the markings of a young theologian! "Do not murder" *is* a good commandment for brothers and sisters. Most of you are probably thinking, "Okay, I've had disagreements with my siblings, but I've never seriously thought about killing them!" If this is what you're thinking, then the contents of this chapter may come as a little surprise to you. Hang on! It's time for a "spiritual" physical!

---

[140] Deut. 5:17.

"Spiritual" Physical

I might as well warn you that this little medical exam may be painful, but in the process remember that the purpose of surgery is to make us healthy. To begin with, like most doctors, I'm going to ask you a few questions about your medical history. First: "Have you ever had a heart transplant?" Second: "Have you ever had a brain transplant?" Third: "Have you ever died?"

Well, how are you doing? If you are a Christian, your answer to each of these questions should have been yes! Allow me to explain. As a believer, the following verses are what the Bible says about your history:

1. *The LORD your God will cleanse your heart and the hearts of all your descendants so that you will love him with all your heart and soul, and so you may live!*[141] *I will give them singleness of heart and put a new spirit within them. I will take away their hearts of stone and give them tender hearts instead.*[142]

So you see, if you are a believer, you have had a heart transplant. Let's look at the other two.

2. *Don't copy the behavior and customs of this world, but let God transform you into a new person by changing the way you think. Then you will know what God wants you to do, and you will know how good and pleasing and perfect his will really is.*[143]

It looks like believers have had a brain transplant as well! God wants to change the way you think.

---

[141] Deut. 30:6.

[142] Ezek. 11:19.

[143] Rom. 12:2.

3. *So you should consider yourselves dead to sin and able to live for the glory of God through Christ Jesus.*[144]

Well, what do you know! The believer is also one who has died!

If you ever want to start, or possibly stop, an interesting conversation with someone, simply tell them that you've had heart and brain transplants and that you have died!

It's Time to Check the Vital Signs

Answering "yes" or "no" to a doctor's questions can be helpful, provided we are telling the truth, but there is also the possibility of thinking we are healthy when in reality we are not. That is why a doctor has to check for signs. It is not only by their testimony that you will know if a person is healthy, but by the evidence.

In the same way, someone may claim to be a Christian and give all the right answers, but that does not necessarily mean that he is a Christian. Jesus said, *"You can detect them by the way they act, just as you can identify a tree by its fruit."*[145] Correct answers are important, but you can tell if a person has surrendered their life to Christ by the way they live.

The Sixth Commandment

So what does all of this have to do with murder? A lot! In John Calvin's Institutes of the Christian Religion, he reminds us that:

When the particular virtue opposed to a particular vice is spoken of, all that is usually meant is abstinence

---

[144] Rom. 6:11.
[145] Matt. 7:16.

from that vice. We maintain that it goes farther, and means opposite duties and positive acts. Hence the commandment, "Thou shall not kill," the generality of (people) will merely consider as an injunction to abstain from all injury, and all wish to inflict injury. I hold that it moreover means, that we are to aid our neighbour's life by every means in our power.[146]

According to Calvin (and Jesus), to not hate means to love, and the key vital sign that someone has had heart and brain transplants and have died is that they love.[147] When Jesus was asked what the greatest of all the commandments was, he replied:

"The most important commandment is this: 'Hear, O Israel! The Lord our God is the one and only Lord. And you must love the Lord your God with all your heart, all your soul, all your mind, and all your strength.' The second is equally important: 'Love your neighbour as yourself.' No other commandment is greater than these."[148]

When Jesus taught specifically on the sixth commandment he said:

"You have heard that the law of Moses says, 'Do not murder. If you commit murder, you are subject to judgment.' But I say, if you are angry with someone, you are subject to judgment! If you call someone an idiot, you are

---

[146] John Calvin, *Institutes of the Christian Religion*, Book 2, edited and translated by Henry Beveridge (Grand Rapids, MI: Eerdmans, 1997) Chapter 8, Section 9.

[147] 1 Cor. 13.

[148] Mark 12:29-31.

*in danger of being brought before the high council. And if
you curse someone, you are in danger of the fires of hell.*"[149]

In the eyes of Jesus, murder is the same as hating
another person, holding on to unresolved anger, cutting
off a friendship because of a disagreement, or wishing for
someone else's failure. Our tongues rather than our guns
have murdered more people. James wrote: *"If you claim to
be religious but don't control your tongue, you are just fooling
yourself, and your religion is worthless."*[150]

John Calvin picks up on this in one of his sermons on
the sixth commandment when he says:

> Our tongue is like a sword. Therefore, although you
> may not have your sword in hand poised to strike, if
> your tongue is armed in such a way as to speak evil
> against (another), and if you have offended (them),
> that is a form of murder in God's sight.[151]

If we are honest we can probably all think of times
we've experienced the cruel words of a teacher, parent,
babysitter, boss, or peer. These words can destroy a
person's image, especially if it happens often enough. God
sees this as murder.

Words carry weight—they can be a source of life or
death. That is why Jesus makes such a serious statement
out of this subject: *"If you curse someone, you are in danger of
the fires of hell.*[152] Those aren't tame words.

---

[149] Matt. 5:21-22.

[150] Jas. 1:26.

[151] John Calvin, *Ten Commandments*; Edited and translated by
Benjamin Farley (Grand Rapids, MI: Baker, 1980) p. 158.

[152] Matt. 5:22.

The Character of God

Jesus is so serious about this because of the close connection it has with God's character. The God who *is* love and community in the Trinity is the God who created us for community—with him and with one another. Love is not something God decided to exhibit—love is who he is![153] That is why the greatest commandment is about love.

To kill community, either physically, emotionally, mentally, or spiritually, is murder. This is why God teaches that when someone murders someone else physically it is the governing authority's responsibility to *"execute anyone who murders another person, for to kill a person is to kill a living being made in God's image."*[154]

Did you catch the reason for the severity of the consequence against physical murder? It is because people have been created in God's image and character. When someone destroys a life they, in a sense, deface the image of the triune God. They destroy and kill someone made in God's image. That is why the reverse is also true. The world will know the true Christians by their love (their community), because that displays the image of God. To kill others (physically, emotionally, spiritually, or mentally) is to blaspheme God.[155]

---

[153] 1 John 4:8.

[154] Gen. 9:6.

[155] That is why a church where people love, forgive, care for, and give up their personal preferences for one another is one of the strongest witnesses in the world. Churches filled with power trips, hypocrisy, gossip, and unforgiveness are the strongest turn off for the world. In fact, the world has the right to question whether or not individuals and churches like this are even Christian. See Francis Schaeffer, *The Mark of the Christian* (IVP; Downers Grove, IL, 1970).

Self Evaluation

Examine yourselves to see if your faith is really genuine. Test yourselves. If you cannot tell that Jesus Christ is among you, it means you have failed the test. I hope you recognize that we have passed the test and are approved by God.[156]

We must ask ourselves some tough questions. Am I building up the community I am a part of, or am I tearing it down? Do the words that I speak to others, and the way I say things at meetings, breathe fresh air, insight, and life into the room, or do my words suck the energy out of the place and cause discouragement and division? When people are around me, do they feel revitalized, or do they need to get away so that they can recharge their batteries?

To think about this from another angle, ask yourself these questions: do I like to be around people who are fun, creative, adventurous, outgoing and full of life, or do I like to be around people who are negative, critical, legalistic, arrogant, and pessimistic? Now, which one are you? Are you a community life giver or a community murderer? Self-evaluation is not easy, but it is necessary.

Right after Jesus taught on the sixth commandment, he said:

"So if you are standing before the altar in the Temple, offering a sacrifice to God, and you suddenly remember that someone has something against you, leave your sacrifice there beside the altar. Go and be reconciled to that person. Then come and offer your sacrifice to God."[157]

---

[156] 2 Cor. 13:5-6.

[157] Matt. 5:23-24.

We cannot worship God with a grudge against another person. Refusing to forgive someone will have a direct effect on our ability to hear from God. After teaching the Lord's Prayer, Jesus said, *"If you forgive those who sin against you, your heavenly Father will forgive you. But if you refuse to forgive others, your Father will not forgive your sins."*[158]

If you are wondering why God is silent in your life, it could be because of this issue. Unforgiveness in your life is like wearing spiritual earplugs. Our ability to correctly interpret the Bible, understand a sermon or a Bible study, and live as a victorious Christian will be greatly hindered when we refuse to forgive. The apostle John says the same thing:

> *If anyone says, "I am living in the light," but hates a Christian brother or sister, that person is still living in darkness. Anyone who loves other Christians is living in the light and does not cause anyone to stumble. Anyone who hates a Christian brother or sister is living and walking in darkness. Such a person is lost, having been blinded by the darkness.*[159]

You should not murder. You should be a life giver! When we obey this commandment, we deepen our relationship with God and our relationships with one another. This shows that we are serious about being a Christian. Jesus' prayer for the future of his church was:

> *"I am praying not only for these disciples but also for all who will ever believe in me because of their testimony. My prayer for all of them is that they will be one, just as you and I are one, Father—that just as you are in me*

---

[158] Matt. 6:14-15.
[159] 1 John 2:9-11.

and I am in you, so they will be in us, and the world will believe you sent me.

"I have given them the glory you gave me, so that they may be one, as we are—I in them and you in me, all being perfected into one. Then the world will know that you sent me and will understand that you love them as much as you love me.[160]

It appears that the boy in that Sunday school class at the beginning of this chapter was correct! "Do not murder" *is* a good commandment for brothers and sisters.

---

[160] John 17:20-23.

CHAPTER EIGHT
Let's Talk About Sex

Do not commit adultery.[161]

Business in the fidelity testing industry is booming. For $500 to $1000 per "situation," wives can employ the likes of Susan Skyy. Susan will then attempt to lure their husbands into an affair so that their wives can see if their husbands will remain faithful. If the husband takes her back to his room, Miss Skyy conveniently receives a message from her boss, makes an excuse to leave, and the man is busted. In explaining the type of "client" Skyy usually works with, she said:

> "Unsuccessful men don't have enough energy to deal with other women in their lives. (The majority of men I deal with are financially well off). They are directors, producers, agents, dot-com people, that sort of thing."[162]

---

[161] Deut. 5:18.

[162] Kate Jennison, "Interested? She's a present. From your suspicious wife: Wherever there is a hotel lobby, gentleman, chances are your wife can arrange for a decoy to 'test' you," *National Post*, Tuesday, April 16, 2002.

Sex has gotten out of control in our society. All we need to do is turn on the television to see that. Sex is everywhere, from the images on billboards, music videos, and movies, to the latest survey and sexual technique "discovered" by *Cosmopolitan*, and to the astronomical rise of Internet pornography, just to name a few places. *Temptation Island* isn't a reality show—it is reality!

At the same time that promiscuous sex has been on the rise, relationships have become increasingly dispensable. Personal pleasure is the be-all-and-end-all. A Christian band I used to listen to in my college days described our societal obsession with sex in one of their songs by asking:

'Isn't sex a wonderful thing?'
Seems like the human race can ruin anything."[163]

God's View On Sex

Sex is not evil; on the contrary, it was created by God and declared "very good."[164] Sex was not the original sin of humanity; disobeying God was.[165] Take food as another example. Like sex, food is not bad. In fact, food is good! Food is enjoyable and brings strength and nourishment to the body. If abused, however, it can lead to gluttony and addiction. The use of food only becomes bad when it is used outside of God's boundaries. It is the same with sexuality. It was only when sin entered time, and we attempted to use God's creation our own way

---

[163] Mad At The World, *Boomerang* (Santa Ana. CA: Alarma Records, 1991): Song *Isn't Sex A Wonderful Thing.* by Roger Rose, Broken Songs, 1991.

[164] Gen. 1:31.

[165] Gen. 2-3.

rather than his way, that we lost control of our desires and passions. God intended sex as a gift to bring us pleasure, intimacy, and children. Through sin, however, we have allowed it to warp lives, bring pain, break relationships, cause revenge, produce guilt, and express itself in perversion. We have fallen from God's ideal of a married man and woman into premarital sex, adulterous affairs, homosexuality, prostitution, incest, sex with children (pedophilia), and bestiality. Jesus reminded us of God's ideal when he said:

> *"Haven't you read the Scriptures? They record that from the beginning 'God made them male and female.' And he said, 'This explains why a man leaves his father and mother and is joined to his wife, and the two are united into one.' Since they are no longer two but one, let no one separate them, for God has joined them together."*[166]

It is in God's ideal that we find good, pleasurable, intimate, fun, and safe sex. God's ways are always best! Even many secular studies have shown that men and women who are faithfully married to one another have the best and the most sex. Once again God gives us a commandment for our protection and pleasure: *"Don't commit adultery."*[167]

The Depths of the Seventh Commandment

In the Sermon on the Mount, Jesus said:

> *"You have heard that the law of Moses says, 'Do not commit adultery.' But I say, anyone who even looks at a*

---

[166] Matt. 19:5-6 (quoting from Gen. 2:20-25).
[167] Deut. 5:18.

woman with lust in his eye has already committed adultery with her in his heart. So if your eye—even if it is your good eye—causes you to lust, gouge it out and throw it away."[168]

When I first become interested in girls, I remember this passage scaring me. I didn't want to become blind. I also didn't want to marry someone I wasn't physically attracted to. How was I to like girls, eventually find one to fall in love with, and *"rejoice in the wife of* [my] *youth…. [Letting]* her breasts satisfy *[me]* always,"[169] while at the same time not even looking at a woman with lust?

What does Jesus mean by *lust*? Does he mean that I cannot even be physically attracted to a woman?[170] In regards to this issue of "adultery of the heart," Dallas Willard gives some advice:

Just as the thief is the person who would steal if circumstances were right, so the adulterer is the one who would have wrongful sex if the circumstances were right. Usually that means if he or she could be sure it would not be found out. This is what Jesus calls "adultery of the heart." In it, the person is not caring for, but using, the other. The condition is wrong even though sexual relations do not occur.[171]

Beyond what Dallas Willard says here, lust is thinking upon, dwelling, and fantasizing about another person sex-

---

[168] Matt. 5:27-29.

[169] Prov. 5:18-19.

[170] Or, for women readers, is it okay to be physically attracted to a man?

[171] Dallas Willard, *The Divine Conspiracy* (New York, NY: HarperSanFrancisco, 1998) p. 161.

ually. This tends to be more of a male issue than a female issue, but both genders do struggle with it. Men and women are sexually charged differently. As a general rule, men are more visually stimulated while women are more emotionally stimulated. That is why a soap opera or cheap romance novel is a greater temptation for a woman, while pornography is a greater temptation for a man, as we will discuss later in this chapter.

A Little Sex Education[172]

Understanding the difference between men and women can enhance the sex life of a married couple. Wives should attempt to be creative and think of different ways they can be visually sexually stimulating for their husbands. Husbands should enhance the sexual aspect of their marriage by spending time communicating, being creatively romantic, and listening to their wives. God's design for sex is that we focus on pleasing our spouse.[173] Unfortunately, what often happens, even among Christians, is that wives will dress up and be sexually appealing when they go out, yet at home, around their spouse, they become frumpy and prudish. In the same way, husbands can give their wives the cold silent treatment and then talk, laugh, and become intellectually stimulating and thoughtful around their secretaries

---

[172] This is certainly not comprehensive and is meant only as a suggestion for married couples, in light of how men and women are generally wired. There are many great books on sexuality by Christian authors that I would recommend married couples read; for example, books by Clifford & Joyce Penner.

[173] Obviously mutual love and respect must be in place. A loving spouse will not force, or make the other person feel guilty about, things one of them may be uncomfortable with.

and female co-workers. Isn't it funny how sin turns every-thing around?

I'm not saying that women should dress poorly in public or that men should not be nice to their female co-workers. What I am saying, especially to Christians, is that within the confines of marriage, where we have been given freedom, we need to learn to be more liberal and to enjoy our freedom. Outside of the marriage context, how-ever, we would all do well to be a bit more conservative. This is the opposite message than what we hear from the world—but why are we listening to the world? What does the world know about sex? It's God who invented it!

Back to Lust and the Seventh Commandment

The opposite of God's design for sex is lust, which is self-focused. "Making love" is about honouring and plea-suring the other person in thought and action, while lust is all about our self. Therefore, there is nothing wrong with being attracted to a member of the opposite sex; however, our thoughts and actions towards them must always be honouring. Sex becomes the greatest honour when we only give it to the one person we have committed our life to. It is just like a secret between two friends, which pulls them closer together. Sex is a special secret between a man and a woman who have publicly vowed to share that secret with each other alone. When we break this confi-dence, by our actions or by our thoughts, we break God's seventh commandment.

The Community Principle

How we behave and restrain ourselves sexually affects the whole community. There are situations, times, and places in which we *should be* sexual, and there are others where we *should not be* sexual. Paul encourages husbands and wives, in the privacy of their *secret,* not to deprive one another sexually,[174] while at the same time he teaches us that in public:

> We should be decent and true in everything we do, so that everyone can approve of our behavior. Don't partic- ipate in wild parties and getting drunk, or in adultery and immoral living, or in fighting and jealousy. But let the Lord Jesus Christ take control of you, and don't think of ways to indulge your evil desires.[175]

Understanding some of the differences between men and women, that were mentioned earlier, can help us be more sexual in the right kinds of situations and less sexual in the wrong situations. We determine this by honouring the other person ahead of ourselves. If men are stimulated visually, women should dress modestly[176] when they are not sharing a secret moment with their husband. For a woman to dress how she wants and then say "men shouldn't look" is a selfish attitude. It puts her and her desires ahead of the men she comes in contact with. In order to honour the men in the community, women need to think about how they dress. Remember, Christianity is about focusing on God and others rather than on self.

In the same way, men should be careful with what they say, entrust, and share with other women. A man should not get too emotionally involved with any woman besides

---

174 1 Cor. 7.

175 Rom. 13:13-14.

176 1 Tim. 2:9-10.

his spouse. Men should be careful regarding the kinds of gifts and messages they may be sending other women—inadvertently or not. For men to say that "women shouldn't read anything into it" is a selfish attitude. When we do this it puts ourselves and our desires ahead of the women we come in contact with.

Lust is about self. Love and sex are about others. Sex is not wrong, but to properly express ourselves sexually, as this commandment teaches, means to think and act appropriately, depending on the context and the situation. There are times to be sexual and there are times not to be—and God has given us the guidelines for our protection and pleasure.

A Special Emphasis for Men

Lust is a huge problem for men. Almost all men claim to struggle with it, and the rest either have the gift of celibacy or are lying! For that reason, I want to say a few more words in relation to this commandment for men. I would still encourage the women to read this section in order to help them understand the struggle most men face. The fact that this is an issue for most men does not give them an excuse for defeat. It is a battle that must be won, and through Christ it can be won!

When the normal visual aspect of a man's sexuality goes unchecked and undisciplined, it can have devastating consequences. Indulgence in pornography is rampant among men, both inside and outside the church. Studies have shown that a large proportion of men sitting in the pews on a Sunday morning are struggling with this issue. In fact, in one survey it was found that 51 percent of *pastors* say that Internet pornography is a temptation for them and 37 percent admitted that it is a current struggle.[177]

The addictive nature of pornography and its "adultery of the heart" has been deadly and has destroyed many men's lives. I have a friend who is a struggling sex addict. It started with pornography and eventually led him to escort services. At one point in his life he was thinking of going into the ministry. Now he is in counselling and hanging on to his marriage. If he were writing this section, I know that he would tell you, as he has told me through tears, "The broken relationships, the shattered dreams, the constant fear of disease is not worth the few moments of empty pleasure."

It is time that we Christian men get serious about this and stop being embarrassed and refusing to talk about it. In the book *Every Man's Battle*, the authors write:

> Before men experience victory over sexual sin, they're hurting and confused. 'Why can't I win at this?' they think. As the fight wears on and the losses pile higher, we begin to doubt everything about ourselves, even our salvation...Where we break down is that we keep praying for deliverance, we plead for someone to remove it. Actually, sexual impurity is a series of bad decisions on our part—a result of immature character—and deliverance won't deliver you into instant maturity. Character work needs to be done...For many men who are willing to fight for sexual purity, an important step is finding accountability.[178]

God is calling us to sexual purity. Jesus pointed out that sexual actions and thoughts that are outside of

---

[177] H.B. London & Neil B. Wiseman, *Pastors at Greater Risk* (Ventura, CA: Regal, 2003) p. 238.

[178] Stephen Arterburn & Fred Stoeker, *Every Man's Battle* (Colorado Springs, CO: WaterBrook, 2000) p. 21, 92 & 115.

God's boundaries are sinful. Obviously there will be much greater consequences for wrongful actions than for wrongful thoughts, but both are missing the mark—and thoughts often lead to action. Illicit sexuality has destroyed many people. In the Bible we are reminded of David and Bathsheba, and Sampson and Delilah. In his thought-provoking book *I was Wrong*, the famous fallen preacher Jim Bakker opens chapter two with the following warning:

> There are many answers to the question "where did things go wrong?" and one answer is my much-publicized encounter with Jessica Hahn. I knew I was wrong the moment I stepped through the door into room 538 at the Sheraton Sand Key Resort in Clearwater Beach, Florida, on December 6, 1980. I never dreamed, however, how much trouble opening that door would cause. Inside that room, I met for the first and only time in my life, a twenty-one-year-old woman named Jessica Hahn.[179]

Victory Can Be Found

Jesus warned us about this strongly when he said, *"If your eye—even if it is your good eye—causes you to lust, gouge it out and throw it away."* Obviously Jesus is not teaching self-mutilation. These are issues of the heart. Jesus often used extreme language to shock his listeners into understanding the severity of the topic he was addressing. Mutilation will not solve the problem. One less eye, or even blindness, doesn't stop someone from lusting. But we may have to "cut off" an environment or

---

[179] Jim Bakker, *I Was Wrong* (Nashville, TN: Nelson, 1996) p. 13.

a relationship that is dangerous and triggers certain temptations.

As Christians we are called to sexual purity. By maintaining an ongoing devotional life with God, having a trusted accountability partner, and avoiding tempting environments and situations, we can be greatly helped in finding victory. It also helps when we live as the community God has called us to be—a people that know when to be sexual and when not to be sexual. We must not take our advice from the world, but from God.

This is not meant to be a "four easy steps to sexual purity" chapter, but hopefully it has given a good starting place. Character development takes time, discipline, and an ongoing relationship with Jesus Christ. If Christ is the Lord of *all*, then he must be the Lord of our sexuality as well as every other part of our life.

God called us to sexual purity when he told us not to commit adultery. God isn't against sex—in fact, *not having sex* (depriving one's spouse) is wrong according to the Bible. There is even a whole book in the Bible about how *good* sex is (*Song of Songs*).

God isn't nearly as embarrassed about sex as we in the church sometimes are. God is, however, disgusted with the way we have perverted sex, which many in the church are not embarrassed enough about. It is funny how God encourages us to go out and have sex, as long as it is within the right context, and we blush and get embarrassed,[180] while the world promotes perversion and many of us sit and watch the sitcoms, movies, and music that promotes it without even blinking an eye!

---

[180] Gen. 1:28.

CHAPTER NINE

Don't Steal

Do not steal.[181]

I remember a time, when I was about six years old, when I stole a little toy from our local convenience store. I also recall my mother dragging me back to that store and forcing me to confess my sin to the manager.

In Augustine's autobiography, he writes of a time in his teenage years when he and some friends stole pears from the neighbour's yard. Reflecting on this he writes:

> The pears I took were O.K., but I had better ones at home. I gathered them only to steal, for as soon as I got them I threw them away—my delight came simply in stealing them.[182]

Some people will go to great lengths to excuse themselves of any wrongdoing in theft. *The Edmonton Journal* printed an article about a man accused of stealing fifty-

---

[181] Deut. 5:19.

[182] Augustine, *Confessions*, II, v. 12.

eight cents from a sport-utility vehicle in June of 1999. The accused took the case to court, and his lawyer subpoenaed the victim's Rottweiler, who was in the car at the time, as a witness. The lawyer said that she "wanted jurors to see how big and ferocious the dog was, suggesting that it made no sense for anyone to break into a vehicle with the dog inside."[183] At the time I read this, taxpayers of Warren County had already shelled out $16,000 towards the case, at a continued cost of $650 an hour.

The eighth commandment teaches us not to steal—yet we often don't get it! Many feel our society has reached enlightenment and an advanced sophistication, yet we still need to remind people with signs that say "Shoplifting is stealing."

Materialism and Stealing

The Western world is materialistic. Let's not deny it or brush over it. It is simply true. This is also a big reason many other countries look upon the West with such hatred. We have a history rooted in greed. When Christopher Columbus landed in the Bahamas, he showed the first natives he came into contact with some gold and asked, "Do you have any of this here?"[184]

We love stuff! We even buy bigger and bigger houses so that we can hoard more and more of our stuff. We buy stuff to protect our stuff. We buy stuff to clean, polish, fix, and improve our stuff. Every summer we ceremoniously

---

[183]"As dog as my witness…: Only in America: a bizarre court case over stolen 58 cents," *The Edmonton Journal*, Thursday, March 29, 2001.

[184] Leonard Sweet, *souLTsunami* (Grand Rapids, MI: Zondervan, 1999) p. 349.

sell our stuff out of our garage, while we drive around and buy other people's stuff out of their garages. After all of this movement and hoarding of stuff comes to an end, it is eventually taken to a great big stuff cemetery where it is ritualistically cremated.

Not only do we like stuff, but a number of us live our lives trying to get more of it. Profession after profession goes on strike for "fairer pay." Radio stations encourage us to call in, say they are the best, and then tell them to "show me my money."[185] Lotteries tell us that the jackpot is now worth six million dollars. Billboards advertise the "sale of the century" if we will just "buy now." Christian celebrities join in and encourage our investment habits if we will just dial 1-800-BUY-COIN. They tell us to pray a prayer for thirty-one days in order for God to enlarge our portfolio. Televangelists rebuke us across the airwaves as being unchristian if we do not send money to support their causes.

In the noise of this, God's commandment tries to get our attention. "Don't steal!" Is anyone listening? "Don't steal!" Stop stealing from God and from others!

Stealing from God

Is it possible to steal from God? God, speaking through the prophet Malachi says, "Yes."

> "Should people cheat God? Yet you have cheated me!
> "But you ask, 'What do you mean? When did we ever cheat you?'
> "You have cheated me of the tithes and offerings due to me. You are under a curse, for your whole nation has been cheating me. Bring all the tithes into the storehouse

---

[185] *Power 92* (92.5 FM) in Edmonton, AB, Canada.

so there will be enough food in my Temple. If you do,"
says the Lord Almighty, "I will open the windows of
heaven for you. I will pour out a blessing so great you
won't have enough room to take it in! Try it! Let me
prove it to you!"[186]

In a study done of eight different Christian denominations, it was found that giving, as a percentage of annual income, decreased from 3.35 percent in 1968 to 2.97 percent in 1993.

[Another] study of eleven denominations between
1921 and 1993 reported that per member giving as a
percentage of income was lower in 1992 than in
1921, and even lower than in 1933, the depth of the
Great Depression.[187]

Churchgoers today are much richer and yet give less.
We *are* materialistic and when God looks at this he calls it
robbery! In fact, the Old Testament teaches that a tithe
should be 10 percent of everything you own and/or
make,[188] and that this should come out of the best you
have (first fruits).[189] The best animals, not the weak and
lame ones, were to be given to God.

In reality, we are only stewards of the things we have,
because everything we own belongs to God. *"The earth is
the Lord's, and everything in it. The world and all its' people*

---

[186] Mal. 3:8-10.

[187] Thomas Reeves, *The Empty Church* (New York, NY: Free Press, 1996) p. 12.

[188] Gen. 14:18-29.

[189] Deut. 18:1-8.

[190] Ps. 24:1.

belong to him."[190] We are called to use the things we have been entrusted with according to the greatest commandment. This means that we are to use them in ways that honour God and others.

What are your attitudes and actions towards your possessions? Are you stealing from God? Are you stealing from others?

Stealing from Others

Paul writes: *"If you are a thief, stop stealing. Begin using your hands for honest work, and then give generously to others in need."*[191]

Stealing from our neighbour involves more than simply stealing money and possessions. We can also rob people of their time and energy. We can deprive people of their liberty. We can withhold opportunities and information from people. *Webster's Dictionary* defines stealing as "personally gaining insidiously or artfully."[192] There are many ways this can be done. Martin Luther reminds us of this in his *Large Catechism* as he writes:

> (This commandment) forbids any conceivable wrong to our neighbour in depriving them of any part of their possessions or interfering with their enjoyment of them; it forbids consent to such wrong, even enjoining all possible prevention; it commands that we add to their possessions and advance their interests.[193]

---

[191] Eph. 4:28.

[192] *Webster's New World Dictionary* (1984).

[193] Martin Luther, *Large Catechism*, Translated by J.N. Lenker (Minneapolis, MI: Augsburg, 1967) p. 59.

To not steal means to actively add and give towards the gain of others. We find this fleshed out in Scripture with some very practical examples:

"When you harvest your crops, do not harvest the grain along the edges of your fields, and do not pick up what the harvesters drop. It is the same with your grape crop—do not strip every last bunch of grapes from the vines, and do not pick up the grapes that fall to the ground. Leave them for the poor and the foreigners who live among you, for I, the Lord, am your God. Do not steal.[194]

God told his people that when they harvested their fields they were to leave the edges and when they picked up grapes in their vineyards they were not to go over them twice. They were to purposely leave the corners of their fields and leftover grapes alone for the poor and the visitors. Again, we read in the Old Testament:

"When you are harvesting your crops and forget to bring in a bundle of grain from your field, don't go back to get it. Leave it for the foreigners, orphans, and widows. Then the LORD your God will bless you in all you do. When you beat the olives from your olive trees, don't go over the boughs twice. Leave some of the olives for the foreigners, orphans, and widows. This also applies to the grapes in your vineyard. Do not glean the vines after they are picked, but leave any remaining grapes for the foreigners, orphans, and widows. Remember that you were slaves in the land of Egypt. That is why I am giving you this command."[195]

---

[194] Lev. 19:9-11.
[195] Deut. 24:19-22.

Not many of us reading this are farmers or harvest vineyards, but the principle implied in these verses is obvious. How would this look today? Maybe putting a cap on what we will live on and giving all the excess to those who are not as fortunate? For example, many authors give all the royalties from their writing to different charities or causes. Maybe the excess of a year-end bonus could be given away to something we feel particularly passionate about. How about giving an overworked waiter a larger-than-they-deserve tip? We could regularly go through our cans and clothes and donate to the food bank or the Salvation Army. We could sponsor a child or ask people to give to an organization in our name rather than get us a Christmas gift. Who needs more stuff at Christmas anyway?

In the Old Testament, hoarding extra for yourself was considered stealing. The Bible teaches equality. Paul writes to different churches encouraging them to apply these principles between themselves.

> *Right now you have plenty and can help them. Then at some other time they can share with you when you need it. In this way, everyone's needs will be met. Do you remember what the Scriptures say about this? "Those who gathered a lot had nothing left over, and those who gathered only a little had enough."*[196]

I'm sure you can be creative and learn not to steal. In fact, consciously deciding to live on less so that more can be given away is a huge testimony of a transformed life in a materialistic and selfish society. It also teaches us to trust God and have a proper focus and motivation for our lives.

---

[196] 2 Cor. 8:14-15.

Jesus said:

> "Can all your worries add a single moment to your life?
> Of course not! And if worry can't do little things like
> that, what's the use of worrying over bigger things?"
>
> "Look at the lilies and how they grow. They don't
> work or make their clothing, yet Solomon in all his glory
> was not dressed as beautifully as they are. And if God
> cares so wonderfully for flowers that are here today and
> gone tomorrow, won't he more surely care for you? You
> have so little faith! And don't worry about food—what
> to eat and drink. Don't worry whether God will provide
> it for you. These things dominate the thoughts of most
> people, but your Father already knows your needs. He
> will give you all you need from day to day if you make
> the Kingdom of God your primary concern."[197]

A Story

The Russian novelist Leo Tolstoy told a story of a man
named Pahom. One day a tribal chief promised Pahom
that he could have all the land that he could walk around
in one day. We read:

> Pahom's eyes glistened: it was all virgin soil, as
> flat as the palm of your hand, as black as the seed of
> a poppy, and in the hollows different kinds of grasses
> grew.
>
> The Chief took off his fox-fur cap, placed it on the
> ground and said:
>
> "This will be the mark. Start from here, and return
> here again. All the land you go around shall be yours."

---

[197] Luke 12:25-31.

Pahom set off at a good pace. He had until sunset that night. After jogging a good distance in one direction he contemplated turning, but felt it was to soon—another three miles could still be taken. Finally he turned and went in another direction and the same scenario played out. He then turned in another direction and did the same. "Just a little farther, just around those trees would be great; it would sure be nice to include that little pool of water," he said to himself.

As the day began to draw to the end, Pahom knew that he had to get back to the spot where the chief had him start in order to close up the land that he had walked around. It was a long way off, and Pahom's feet were worn and he was weary from his travel, but he began to sprint with the little energy he had left. He tripped, banged up his knees, and began to spit up blood, but he was determined to make it back to the start. The sun was close to the rim and about to set.

With all his remaining strength he rushed on, bending his body forward so that his legs could hardly follow fast enough to keep him from falling again…. He reached a hill and looked up at the sun—the sun (appeared to have) already set! He gave a cry, "All my labour has been in vain."

He took a breath and ran up the hill. It was still light on the other side. He ran and ran, he could see the Chief, the sun was now almost out of sight. As the last bit of light from the sun disappeared Pahom's legs gave way beneath him, he fell forward and reached the cap with his hands.

"Ah, that's a fine fellow!" exclaimed the Chief. "He has gained much land!"

Pahom's servant came running up and tried to raise him, but he saw that blood was flowing from his mouth. Pahom was dead!

His servant picked up the spade and dug a grave long enough for Pahom to lie in and buried him in it. Six feet from his head to his heels was all the land he needed.[198]

Conclusion

How much stuff is enough? How much money is enough? How much land does a person need?

When asked these questions, John Rockefeller Sr. said, "Just a little bit more."

When asked these questions the wealthy King Solomon wrote:

"Everything is meaningless, utterly meaningless!" What do people get for all their hard work? Everything is so weary and tiresome! No matter how much we see, we are never satisfied. No matter how much we hear, we are not content.

I also tried to find meaning by building huge homes for myself and by planting beautiful vineyards. I made gardens and parks, filling them with all kinds of fruit trees. I built reservoirs to collect the water to irrigate my many flourishing groves. I bought slaves, both men and women, and others were born into my household. I also owned great herds and flocks, more than any of the kings who lived in Jerusalem before me. I collected great sums

---

[198] Leo Tolstoy, *How Much Land Does a Man Need?*: Os Guinness (Ed), *Steering Through Chaos* (Colorado Springs, CO: NavPress, 2000) pp. 182-197.

of silver and gold, the treasure of many kings and provinces. I hired wonderful singers, both men and women, and had many beautiful concubines. I had everything a man could desire!

Anything I wanted, I took. I did not restrain myself from any joy. But as I looked at everything I had worked so hard to accomplish, it was all so meaningless. It was like chasing the wind. There was nothing really worthwhile anywhere.[199]

When asked these questions, Jesus said, *"How do you benefit if you gain the whole world but lose your own soul in the process?"*[200]

When asked these questions, God said, "Don't steal!"

When we love God and others, stealing is out of the question. Instead, love leads to an attitude of giving. We cannot steal from God if we love him. Instead, we want to give God even more of our time, our talents, and our treasures. We cannot steal from our neighbours if we love them. Instead we help, encourage, and give to our neighbours!

"Don't steal." It's for our, and our neighbours', protection and pleasure.

---

[199] Eccl. 1:1-2, 8; 2:4-8, 10-11.
[200] Matt. 16:26.

CHAPTER TEN
Don't Lie

Do not testify falsely against your neighbor.[201]

The ninth commandment teaches, *"Do not testify falsely against your neighbor."* In other words, "Do not lie!" I once had someone tell me that Christians don't tell lies—they sing them. If we were honest about what we sing in church a number of the songs in our hymnals would have to change their lyrics. Some of these "honest" hymns would have titles like, "I Surrender Some," "Fill Up My Spoon, Lord," "Oh, How I Like Jesus," "I Love To Talk About Telling The Story," "Take My Life And Let Me Be," "It's My Secret What God Can Do," "Where He Leads Me, I Will Consider Following," 'Just as I Pretend To Be," and "When The Saints Go Sneaking In."

Lies are easy to tell—and to sing. We tell our spouse one thing and do another. We make promises to our children, but don't keep them. We record more hours at work then we put in. We tell our neighbours that the fence will cost more than it does. We say everything is okay when we

---

[201] Deut. 5:20.

are broken on the inside. We fudge on our taxes, and we tell ourselves that we are not liars.

Lying to Others and Lying to God

Even though this commandment deals with lying about others or lying to others, we can also lie to God. In fact, we will see that these are interconnected. For example, in Acts 5 we have the story of Ananias and Sapphira. Very early in the church's history, after the coming of the Holy Spirit,[202] the church took a crack at communism.[203] We read:

> *All the believers were of one heart and mind, and they felt that what they owned was not their own; they shared everything they had. And the apostles gave powerful witness to the resurrection of the Lord Jesus, and God's great favor was upon them all. There was no poverty among them, because people who owned land or houses sold them and brought the money to the apostles to give to others in need.*[204]

When Ananias and Sapphira enter the story, we are told that they also sold some property. We read that Ananias *"brought part of the money to the apostles, but he claimed it was the full amount. His wife had agreed to this deception."*[205] Ananias lied to the apostles, telling them that

---

[202] Early 30s AD.

[203] It didn't work then either. We later see Paul advocating help for the poor church in Jerusalem after it "sold all it had and shared everything equally" (Romans 16:25-28).

[204] Acts 4:32-35.

[205] Acts 5:2.

the money he was giving them was the full amount. Filled with God's Spirit, Peter knew exactly what Ananias and Sapphira had done, and said to them:

"Ananias, why has Satan filled your heart? You lied to the Holy Spirit, and you kept some of the money for yourself. The property was yours to sell or not sell, as you wished. And after selling it, the money was yours to give away. How could you do a thing like this? You weren't lying to us but to God."[206]

According to Peter's assessment, lying to others is the same as lying to God. Lying doesn't fool God, for God knows all things. God knows what we are doing at all times. *"When the Lord comes, he will bring our deepest secrets to light and will reveal our private motives."*[207]

God is not duped by our lies, even though he may ask us a rhetorical question in order to help us discover our sin, as God did through Peter to Ananias. He does this to allow us to repent. God knows the truth.

In a very humorous denial of God's ability to know all things,[208] Charles Templeton writes about the account in the Garden of Eden found in Genesis 3:8-9. He says:

God is not omniscient: Out for an evening stroll in the garden, he seems to have no idea where the first man and woman are hiding and has to ask where they are and what they have been up to.[209]

---

[206] Acts 5:3-4.

[207] 1 Cor. 4:5.

[208] This ability of God has been given the term *omniscience*.

[209] Charles Templeton, *Farewell to God* (Toronto, ON: McClelland & Stewart, 1996) p. 46.

It is hard for me to take this as a serious argument. Of course God knew where Adam and Eve were. The question "where are you?" is much more of a spiritual question than a question about physical location, and God already knows the answer to even this spiritual question. Why Templeton would see this as proof that God doesn't know all things baffles me. Questions are   asked every day by people who already know the answer. Have you every had a police officer ask you, "Do you know how fast you were going?" In the classroom teachers are always asking questions that they know the answers to, and preachers often sprinkle their sermons with rhetorical questions. These questions are asked for the sake of the student, not the teacher. In the same way, when God asks us a question (like he did with Adam and Eve and Ananias and Sapphira), it is not because he is ignorant but because we are.

Ananias and Sapphira lied about how much they gave. Adam and Eve messed up and then tried to hide in the bushes. Aaron built a golden calf[210] for the people to worship, and then, when he got in trouble, said, "I just put the gold in the pot and out came this calf."[211] Isaac tries to save his hide by telling Abimelech that Rebekah was his sister and then gets caught making out with her.[212]

We lie to others and we lie to God. Then God shows up for our protection and pleasure and asks, "Where are you?

---

[210] See Exodus 32 if you are unfamiliar with the story of the golden calf.

[211] Ex. 33:24.

[212] Gen. 26:7-10.

What are you doing with your life? Where are you going?" and some of us answer, "God is sure stupid! He doesn't even know where I am!"

In the same way, Peter asks Sapphira, "Tell me, is this the price you and Ananias got for the land?" Peter obviously knows the answer; not only did the Holy Spirit reveal it to him, but her husband just dropped dead a few hours earlier for lying about the same thing. Ananias came to church expecting to receive the "tithe of the month" award but ended up leaving in a body bag.

> As soon as Ananias heard these words, he fell to the floor and died. Everyone who heard about it was terrified. Then some young men wrapped him in a sheet and took him out and buried him.[213]

Lying is pretty serious. From this New Testament story we can learn a few things about the ninth commandment.

1. When we lie to others, we lie to God.

2. God is not stupid—he knows all things and he knows when we are lying. It is futile to try and trick him.

3. God tries to get our attention through asking questions. (Where are you?)

4. The price of lying and resisting God's questions is death.

What would have happened if Ananias and Sapphira had confessed their sin when Peter first asked them? What would have happened if Adam and Even had confessed

---

[213] Acts 5:5-6.

their sin when God asked them? I guess we will never know in those cases, but when God asks us the questions, we can tell the truth and find out for ourselves.

Peter said to Sapphira, *"Just outside that door are the young men who buried your husband, and they will carry you out, too."*[214] That's a pretty freaky Steven-King-kind-of-thing to say!

> *Instantly, she fell to the floor and died. When the young men came in and saw that she was dead, they carried her out and buried her beside her husband. Great fear gripped the entire church and all others who heard what had happened.*[215]

God is to be loved, but he is also to be feared. There has been a great neglect in teaching the fact that God is *also* wrathful toward wrongdoing and a punisher of sin. A liar *will* face the music.

Facing the Music

I heard a story[216] of a man who conned his way into the orchestra of the emperor of China, even though he couldn't play a single note. Whenever the group practiced or performed, he would hold his flute against his lips and pretend to play but not make a sound. By doing this he received a modest salary and enjoyed a comfortable living. One day, however, the emperor requested a solo from each musician. Hearing this, the flutist got (understandably) nervous. With not enough time to learn the instrument, he pretended to be

---

[214] Acts 5:9.

[215] Acts 5:10-11.

[216] I don't know if it is true or not.

sick, but he couldn't fool the royal physician. When the day of his solo performance arrived, he took poison and killed himself. It is from this story that the phrase "he refused to face the music" found its way into the English language.

God punishes because he loves. God asks us where we are because he desires to save us. How do we respond? We can lie. We can convince ourselves to believe an untruth. We can live our whole lives running from God and attempting to fool everyone around us. Or, we could learn to fear God and acknowledge that living in sin only wrecks our lives and the lives of others. We might not instantly drop dead as Ananias and Sapphira did, but sin does kill us. A lying life (or a life that is a lie) slowly slips into a meaningless, empty existence.

You cannot live a lie forever. Eventually it will be exposed. Eventually you will face the music. Lying destroys our relationships with God and others. It destroys trust, reality, beauty, faith, hope, and love. "Don't lie"—it's not good for you.

The Father of Lies

Of course Satan doesn't want us to be protected and have pleasure, so he attempts to twist these commandments by saying that in breaking them we will find true freedom and enjoyment. This ninth commandment strikes at the heart of Satan's character. He lies about God and his commandments in order to harm us. In doing so he breaks the ninth commandment in order to tempt us to break all the others. God is truth and Satan is a liar (a twister of truth). In fact, the Bible refers to Satan as the "father of lies." Speaking to those who break God's commandments but lie and convince themselves that they are actually obeying them, Jesus said:

For you are the children of your father the Devil, and you love to do the evil things he does. He was a murderer from the beginning and has always hated the truth. There is no truth in him. When he lies, it is consistent with his character; for he is a liar and the father of lies. So when I tell the truth, you just naturally don't believe me![217]

Did you notice how Satan is described as a murderer *and* a liar? That is because sin and death go together. Physical, emotional, relational, mental, and spiritual death are a result of lies and of a life lived outside of the truth. It is no wonder this showed up in the ten commandments.

The God of Truth

"Do not testify falsely against your neighbour."[218] To bear false testimony is to live a lie. It is to acknowledge Satan as your father rather than God as your Father. God's people are opposed to any and every form of deception. We are called to be a people of truth, of light, and of life because we follow the one who is the Way, the Truth, and the Life.[219] In fact, Jesus began many of his teachings with the phrase, "I tell you the truth."[220] He also said: *"You are truly my disciples if you keep obeying my teachings. And you will know the truth, and the truth will set you free."*[221]

Satan is a liar and a murderer. Jesus is the Truth and the Life. Lies bring death. Truth brings life. When we tes-

---

[217] John 8:44-45.

[218] Deut. 5:20.

[219] John 14:6.

[220] i.e., John 5:19; 6:26, 32, 53; 8:34, 58; 10:1, 7, etc. (see *New International Version*).

[221] John 8:31-32.

tify falsely against God and others, we break relationship with them. As Christians, we have been called to be a people of truth and of wholeness. We have become part of a new community of truth. As Paul writes:

> With the Lord's authority let me say this: Live no longer as the ungodly do, for they are hopelessly confused. Their closed minds are full of darkness; they are far away from the life of God because they have shut their minds and hardened their hearts against him. They don't care anymore about right and wrong, and they have given themselves over to immoral ways. Their lives are filled with all kinds of impurity and greed.
>
> But that isn't what you were taught when you learned about Christ. Since you have heard all about him and have learned the truth that is in Jesus, throw off your old evil nature and your former way of life, which is rotten through and through, full of lust and deception. Instead, there must be a spiritual renewal of your thoughts and attitudes. You must display a new nature because you are a new person, created in God's likeness—righteous, holy, and true.
>
> So put away all falsehood and "tell your neighbour the truth" because we belong to each other.[222]

Since Jesus is the Truth, his people are to live in the truth. "Do not testify falsely against your neighbour"[223] is about more than just lying. It is a whole philosophy of life. The children of the Truth shall live by the truth!

---

[222] Eph. 4:17-25.

[223] Deut. 5:20.

CHAPTER ELEVEN
Don't Be Greedy

> *Do not covet your neighbor's wife.*
> *Do not covet your neighbor's house or land,*
> *male or female servant, ox or donkey,*
> *or anything else your neighbor owns.*[224]

The T-shirt cost $190 and she just had to have it. Not just one, but three—one in each color. Nancy Osbourn, 44, and mother of two, said in the *Edmonton Sun:* "I need fixes. When I'm happy, I buy even more. I get instant gratification."[225]

Although Ms. Osbourn denies being one, shopaholism is a growing phenomenon. Unlike other addictions, a University of Toronto sociologist says shopaholism "is more acceptable because we live in a consumer culture."[226]

I gotta have it! Give me, give me! Mine, mine, mine! These words of a four year old have become the accepted words of forty-four year olds.

The last commandment reads: *"Do not covet your neighbour's wife. Do not covet your neighbour's house or land, male or female servant, ox or donkey, or anything else your neighbour owns. "*

---

[224] Deut. 5:21.

[225] *Edmonton Sun,* "Just Gotta Have It!", Mar. 19, 2001, p. 38.

[226] Ibid.

In other words: Do not covet your neighbour's wife (or husband). Do not covet your neighbour's house or land, (their landscaping services or their house cleaning services, their Porsche or BMW), or anything else your neighbour owns.

Like all the rest, this is a very counter-cultural commandment!

A Story

In one of C.S. Lewis' classic *Tales of Narnia*, the ship *The DawnTreader* stops at an unknown island. The crew, Caspian, Edmund, Lucy, the talking mouse Reepicheep, and others, go ashore to look around. There they discover a lake, and being a hot day they decide to jump in, refresh themselves, and have a drink. Just as the boy Eustace is about to scoop some of the water with his hands, Lucy and Reepicheep cry out. At the bottom of the pool there is a life-size statue of a man, made entirely of gold. He is laying face downward with his arms stretched above his head.

> "Well!" whistled Caspian. "That was worth coming to see! I wonder, can we get it out?"
>
> "We can dive for it, sire," said Reepicheep.
>
> "No good at all," said Edmund. "It will be far too heavy to bring up. (And the pool is fairly deep). It's a good thing I've brought a hunting spear with me. Let's see what the depth is like. Hold on to my hand, Caspian, while I lean out over the water a bit." Caspian took his hand and Edmund, leaning forward, began to lower his spear into the water.
>
> Before it was halfway in Lucy said, "I don't believe the statue is gold at all. It's only light. Your spear looks just the same colour."

"What's wrong?" asked several voices at once, for Edmund had suddenly let go of the spear.

"I couldn't hold it," gasped Edmund, "it seemed so heavy."

"And there it is on the bottom now," said Caspian, "and Lucy is right. It looks just the same colour as the statue."

But Edmund, who appeared to be having some trouble with his boots—at least he was bending down and looking at them—straightened himself all at once and shouted out in the sharp voice which people hardly ever disobey:

"Get back! Back from the water! All of you! At once!!"[227]

It seems that the pool in this tale from Narnia had a "Midas touch." The desire to retrieve the gold statue at the bottom of the lake and cash in on its wealth almost turned fatal. In the same way, our desires, if not kept in control, can be the death of us. So God says, "Don't covet." This commandment is warning us to "get back" and look deep into our hearts. What are my desires and pursuits? Are they leading me to life or to death?

Some Misconceptions About Desire

What is wrong with desire? Truthfully, nothing! In fact, God created our desires. God created our desire for food, for warmth, for sleep, for love, for sex, for friendship, for stability, for work, and for a relationship with him. These all come from God. As we have said throughout this book,

---

[227] C.S. Lewis, *Voyage of the Dawn Treader* (Canada: Fontana/Lions, 1952) pp. 98-99.

God wants us to enjoy pleasure. That is why he gave us these guidelines—so that we could find true pleasure and be protected from false pleasure.

This commandment is not speaking against desires but against wrongly placed and misguided desires. For example, we can take our godly desire for rest (Sabbath) and become lazy. We can take our God-given desire for sex and lust after and engage in sex outside of a married relationship. We can take our God-given desire for food and become a glutton. We can take our God-given desire for a relationship with him and worship false gods.

Augustine observed that evil is not a self-created entity but is only goodness that has been twisted and warped. The consequence of our distorting goodness is an emptying of our true personhood. Sin is not what makes us human but what makes us less than human. The more we twist good things (sin), the more we experience death. In the same way, the more we live up to God's standards and principles of righteousness the more we experience life.[228]

"Do not desire the things I have put off limits," God warns, "for in doing this you will only destroy yourselves."[229] When we sin and chase after the things God has put out-of-bounds we ruin our lives. Therefore, get back! Get back from the water! All of you! At once!

Going Further

This commandment against coveting is more than a warning about the danger of giving in to wrong desires. As we have already seen, in each of these chapters on the

---

[228] Rom. 6:23.
[229] Rom. 1:24-32.

commandments, God not only teaches us to avoid such things as stealing, killing, and lying, but he has also taught us to put to death the wrong desire itself. In fact, as Jesus taught us in the Sermon on the Mount,[230] having the desire to do something wrong is sin. The consequences might not be as great as actually doing it, but it still qualifies us as less-than-perfect individuals who fall below God's perfect standards.[231] The severity of this has sent many Christians into self-defeating downward spirals of self-examination. We try to stop having wrong desires, but the very attempt at trying not to think about such things causes us to think about them even more. Down and down we go. These commandments are hard enough, but this last commandment makes it simply impossible. Paul recognized this and wrote these autobiographical words:

> Yet I could have confidence in myself if anyone could. If others have reason for confidence in their own efforts, I have even more! For I was circumcised when I was eight days old, having been born into a pure-blooded Jewish family that is a branch of the tribe of Benjamin. So I am a real Jew if there ever was one! What's more, I was a member of the Pharisees, who demand the strictest obedience to the Jewish law. And zealous? Yes, in fact, I harshly persecuted the church. And I obeyed the Jewish law so carefully that I was never accused of any fault.[232]

If anyone could get to heaven by good hard work, Paul would have been a top candidate. When it came to

---

[230] Matt. 5-7.

[231] Rom. 3:20; 23.

[232] Phil. 3:4-6.

keeping the commandments, Paul thought his score was pretty good. Then Paul realized that the breaking of the last commandment meant that he had really broken all of the others—at least in thought.

Well then, am I suggesting that the law of God is evil? Of course not! The law is not sinful, but it was the law that showed me my sin. I would never have known that coveting is wrong if the law had not said, **"Do not covet."** *But sin took advantage of this law and aroused all kinds of forbidden desires within me! If there were no law, sin would not have that power.*[233]

The Law—A Good Doctor

The law is not sin, but the law exposes the sin within us. The law is like a good doctor who points out to you that you have cancer. This is a good thing! It is not good news, but it is good and necessary to know. Ignorance may give us a kind of pseudo-comfort, but the cancer will still kill us, and we will not have been able to do anything to try and stop it. It is better to know about the cancer and try and do something about it (or learn to deal with it) than to not know at all.

In the same way, Paul realizes that the law has shown him his sickness (sinfulness). Paul sees this as good. "If it was not for this tenth commandment," Paul writes, "I would still be lost in my sin. This commandment revealed to me that I am a sinner and that I need a Savior."

This last commandment deals with the sinful attitudes of our heart. God is not mocking us but allowing us to realize the depth of our sin in the hopes that we will do

---

[233] Rom. 7:7-8, emphasis mine.

something about it by calling out to him. It is not that God has set the standard so high but that we have sunk so low from God's original plan.[234] Our thoughts, desires, and emotions—our *very* beings (souls) have fallen and become sinful.

Grace—Our Good Saviour

This is not a reason for despair, because there is a way back to life. Paul does say in Romans, *"for all have sinned; all fall short of God's glorious standard,"*[235] but the message doesn't end there. Paul also goes on to say:

Yet now God in his gracious kindness declares us not guilty. He has done this through Christ Jesus, who has freed us by taking away our sins. For God sent Jesus to take the punishment for our sins and to satisfy God's anger against us. We are made right with God when we believe that Jesus shed his blood, sacrificing his life for us.[236]

So the answer is not found in giving up, but in giving up our lives to Christ. About this Jesus, Paul writes in another place:

Though he was God, he did not demand and cling to his rights as God. He made himself nothing; he took the humble position of a slave and appeared in human form. And in human form he obediently humbled himself even further by dying a criminal's death on a cross. Because of this, God raised him up to the heights of heaven and gave him a name that is above every other name, so that at the

---

[234] Gen. 3.

[235] Rom. 3:23.

[236] Rom. 3:24-25.

name of Jesus every knee will bow, in heaven and on earth and under the earth, and every tongue will confess that Jesus Christ is Lord, to the glory of God the Father.[237]

Only Christ can put to death those areas of sin and struggle in our lives and bring about new life. He can do this because he paid the sin penalty and rose from the dead. How we begin being transformed into command-ment keepers does not come from inside ourselves but from outside of ourselves. It comes about through surren-dering to Christ, when we die to ourselves (our false selves) and let Christ indwell us.[238] Once this happens a true inside-out process can begin. Our hearts begin to change and we become more and more genuine. This can only happen when we encounter the living person of Jesus Christ. Then the truly unbelievable begins to take shape.

Living Proof

The *Wall Street Journal* called it "an extraordinary renunciation of materialism." In 1960, for $900, Tom Monaghan and his brother James bought a home-delivery pizza service called Domi-Nick's. After a year James swapped his half with his brother Tom for a Volkswagen Beetle. Tom Monaghan then changed the name to Domino's and went on to build a mega-corporation with 6,100 outlets worldwide, becoming a billionaire.

Today, however, Tom has sold most of his interest in Domino's. He has parted with his yacht, aircraft, radio sta-tion, vintage car collection, the Detroit Tigers baseball team, and his Lake Huron resort. When asked why, Tom

---

[237] Phil. 2:6-11.
[238] Gal. 2:20.

simply replied, "They were a distraction." He then went on to sell all his worldly goods, gave most of the money to charity, and is spending what remains of his life and wealth building Catholic schools across the United States.

What happened? Friends say that a book called *Mere Christianity* by C.S. Lewis heavily influenced him. Explaining himself in *The Telegraph*, he said, "I realized how bad a person I really am. It was exciting, because it showed I really have got some chance of improvement."[239]

Another individual described himself as Calgary's king of second-hand pornography. His name is Harold Harcus and he used to run Dr. Hook's Used Tapes and Books on Macleod Trail. A year and a half before this article was written, a friend invited him to come to church. "Just walking up the stairs changed my life," he said, "I felt the Spirit of God within me. Once I started going to church, I realized that what I was doing was not right. It's not what God wanted."

The following Sunday he and the congregation, led by Pastor Don Delaney, celebrated by shredding 30,000 magazines and smashing hundreds of pornographic videos.[240]

Some people really do "sell all they have" when they come to Christ![241] Did you notice how the turn around came for both Tom and Harold? They came to realize their sinfulness. Like Paul, it didn't lead them to despair but to

---

[239] Ted and Virginia Byfield, "Orthodoxy—Sometimes the Wealthy actually do Sell everything and give to the Poor," Link Byfield (Ed). *Alberta Report*, Edmonton, AB; Oct. 26, 1998, p. 38.

[240] Ted and Virginia Byfield, "Orthodoxy—While Liberal Clerics deplore Conversion, Jan Fonda and a Calgary Porn King defy them," Link Byfield. *The Report*, Edmonton, AB, July 24, 2000, p. 46.

[241] Luke 18:18-30.

Christ! When we start down that road of surrender to Christ, our entire life turns upside down (or should I say right-side up?).

What a contrast we see between Tom Monaghan, who sold all he had and gave the proceeds to charity, and Harold Harcus, who destroyed his pornography business, and Nancy Osbourn, who excused buying three T-shirts for $570 by saying, "I need fixes. When I'm happy, I buy even more. I get instant gratification."

The question that each of us in the North American church must ask ourselves is, "Why do so many of us look more like Nancy Osbourn than Tom Monaghan or Harold Harcus?" God said: "Do not covet your neighbour's wife (or husband). Do not covet your neighbour's house or land, (their landscaping services) or (their house cleaning services) (their Porsche or BMW), or anything else your neighbour owns."

CHAPTER TWELVE
The Most Important Thing

Jesus often spoke to and debated with the crowds. On one occasion a certain teacher of the law stood back and listened intently. When he began to realize that Jesus spoke with authority and answered with profound wisdom he decided to ask Jesus a question of his own. *"Of all the commandments, which is the most important?"*[242] In other words, "How can I please God with my life by obeying the most important commandment?"

This teacher of the law knew that around 1400 years ago a man by the name of Moses went up Mt. Sinai and had a forty-day encounter with God, out of which came the ten commandments. But this teacher also knew that these ten commandments were just God's basic requirement; in actuality, scholars and historians have counted 613 different laws in the five books attributed to

---

[242] Mark 12:28.

Moses.[243] So the question is a fitting one, "Of all these commandments, which one is the most important one?" Jesus answered:

> *"The most important commandment is this: 'Hear, O Israel! The Lord our God is the one and only Lord. And you must love the Lord your God with all your heart, all your soul, all your mind, and all your strength.' The second is equally important: 'Love your neighbour as yourself.' No other commandment is greater than these."*[244]

The Character of God

It is significant that Jesus begins to answer this question about the greatest commandment with the theological affirmation "The Lord is the one and only Lord" and then goes on to say that the greatest commandment is love for God and love for our neighbour. The *New Living Translation* is a bit incomplete here. Most translations say something like, "Hear, O Israel! The Lord our God, the Lord is one!" This is more accurate and says more than the fact that God is the one and only. It also implies that God is one essence. This is important, as it roots the commandment that Jesus gives in theology about the character of God.

The Lord is One

God is three persons, yet one essence.[245] This doctrine, known as the Trinity, is not philosophical mumbo-jumbo

---

[243] These are the first five books of the Old Testament, known by Jews as the Torah: Genesis, Exodus, Leviticus, Numbers, and Deuteronomy.

[244] Mark 12:29-31.

[245] The standard orthodox position of the church as affirmed in the Nicene Creed.

but describes to us the character of God. The Bible not only teaches us that God loves but that God *is* love.[246] The very *essence* of God is love, as the eternal Father, eternal Son, and eternal Holy Spirit exist in an eternal love relationship. Love always was, is, and will be, between the three persons of God.

So, when asked what the greatest commandment was, Jesus said, "God is the one and only, and God is one unified essence of love, therefore, the greatest commandment is for you to *love* God and *love* one another." Let's unpack this.

1. Jesus didn't arbitrarily pull this commandment out of the air but based it on the nature of God's character.

As already stated, the greatest commandment is to love God and others, because the nature of God is a perfect love relationship reflected in the Trinity. Therefore, loving God and loving one another expresses the very purpose for which we have been created. It answers our "why" questions. Why shouldn't I steal? Why shouldn't I kill? Why shouldn't I lie? Answer: because, when you *love* others you don't do those things to them. Notice the contrast, between those who live by the greatest commandment and understand the "why" and those who simply try to live for themselves, in the following excerpt from a letter Sigmund Freud wrote to J. J. Putnam:

> When I ask myself why I have always aspired to behave honourably, to spare others and be kind whenever possible, and why I didn't cease doing so when I realised that in this way one comes to harm

---

[246] 1 John 4:8.

and becomes an anvil because other people are brutal and unreliable, then indeed I have no answer.[247]

As Christians, we obey the commandments because they teach us how to love. The reason we strive to love is because the God in whose image we have been created[248] is a God of love.

2. Jesus didn't give a new law, but a renewed understanding of the law.

Both commands to love God and to love our neighbour are found in the books of Moses (the Torah). The commandment to love God is found in Deuteronomy 6:4-5 and the commandment to love our neighbour is found in Leviticus 19:18. Jesus is not teaching something new or saying that this commandment overrides the other commands. He is saying that this commandment fulfills the other ones. To love God and love our neighbour is the very heart of the law. It explains the purpose of the other laws. In fact, the ten commandments are simply commentary on *how* to love God and others.

3. Jesus saw love for God and for our neighbour as the greatest commandment (singular).

To love God only is mysticism and not really love at all. To only love people is secular humanism and, equally, not real love. Jesus said that there was no greater *commandment* (singular) than *both* loving God and loving others. The two commandments are, in a sense, one com-

---

[247] Hans Kung, *On Being A Christian* (Great Britain, Glasgow: Fount, 1978) p. 683.

[248] Gen. 1:27.

mandment. When we do the one, we, in fact, do the other. To love God and to love others is true love. That is what Jesus meant when he said:

> *"Then these righteous ones will reply, 'Lord, when did we ever see you hungry and feed you? Or thirsty and give you something to drink? Or a stranger and show you hospitality? Or naked and give you clothing? When did we ever see you sick or in prison, and visit you?' And the King will tell them, 'I assure you, when you did it to one of the least of these my brothers and sisters, you were doing it to me!'"*[249]

Mother Teresa echoed these words when she said:

> Jesus comes to meet us. To welcome him, let us go meet him. He comes to us in the hungry, the naked, the lonely, the alcoholic, the drug addict, the prostitute, the street beggars. He may come to you or me in a father who is alone, in a mother, in a brother, or in a sister. If we reject them, if we do not go out to meet them, we reject Jesus himself.[250]

How do we love our neighbour? We love God! How do we love God? We love our neighbour! Who is my neighbour?

> *Jesus replied with an illustration: "A Jewish man was traveling on a trip from Jerusalem to Jericho, and he was attacked by bandits. They stripped him of his clothes and money, beat him up, and left him half dead beside the road.*

---

[249] Matt. 25:37-40.

[250] Mother Teresa, *In My Own Words*: Compiled by Jose Luis Gonzalez-Balado (New York, NY: Gramercy, 1996) p. 29.

"By chance a Jewish priest came along; but when he saw the man lying there, he crossed to the other side of the road and passed him by. A Temple assistant walked over and looked at him lying there, but he also passed by on the other side.

"Then a despised Samaritan came along, and when he saw the man, he felt deep pity. Kneeling beside him, the Samaritan soothed his wounds with medicine and bandaged them. Then he put the man on his own donkey and took him to an inn, where he took care of him. The next day he handed the innkeeper two pieces of silver and told him to take care of the man. 'If his bill runs higher than that,' he said, 'I'll pay the difference the next time I am here.'

"Now which of these three would you say was a neighbour to the man who was attacked by bandits?" Jesus asked.

The man replied, "The one who showed him mercy."

Then Jesus said, "Yes, now go and do the same." [251]

In fact, Jesus went so far as to say:

"You have heard that the law of Moses says, 'Love your neighbour' and hate your enemy. But I say, love your enemies! Pray for those who persecute you!" [252]

What Jesus said here is impossible to live out with our own abilities, but with God all things are possible. [253] As Christians, Christ can and does transform our hearts and minds. Christ can and does empower us with his Holy

---

[251] Luke 10:30-37.

[252] Matt. 5:43-44.

[253] Luke 18:27.

Spirit to live by the power of God's love—which is so much wider, longer, higher, and deeper[254] than the narrowness of our own love. In fact, when we surrender our wills to Christ he comes and takes over our lives and lives in and through us.[255]

The teacher of the law who asked Jesus the question about the greatest commandment was perceptive. After he heard Jesus' answer he said:

> "Well said, Teacher. You have spoken the truth by saying that there is only one God and no other. And I know it is important to love him with all my heart and all my understanding and all my strength, and to love my neighbours as myself. This is more important than to offer all of the burnt offerings and sacrifices required in the law."[256]

4. The greatest of these is love (Mark 12:32-33).

To love God and others *is more important* than all the burnt offerings and sacrifices. What a radical statement for a Jewish teacher of the law to make. At this point some of his colleagues probably began to suspect him of heresy. We lose some of the power of his statement because of the cultural distance, but what this teacher of the law is saying is equivalent to, "Love for God and others is more important than singing hymns or choruses in church, more important than hours of intercessory prayer, more important than reading your Bible and listening to sermons." Not that

---

[254] Eph. 4:18.

[255] Gal. 2:20.

[256] Mark 12:32-33.

these things aren't important and necessary for spiritual growth, but without love they amount to nothing. Paul said the same thing to the Corinthians:

> If I could speak in any language in heaven or on earth but didn't love others, I would only be making meaningless noise like a loud gong or a clanging cymbal. If I had the gift of prophecy, and if I knew all the mysteries of the future and knew everything about everything, but didn't love others, what good would I be? And if I had the gift of faith so that I could speak to a mountain and make it move, without love I would be no good to anybody. If I gave everything I have to the poor and even sacrificed my body, I could boast about it; but if I didn't love others, I would be of no value whatsoever…. There are three things that will endure—faith, hope, and love—and the greatest of these is love.[257]

Love God and Do as You Please

St. Augustine once said, "Love God and do as you please," and he was right. When we love God we can do as we please, because what pleases us is pleasing the one we love. When we love, the commandments are not seen as a set of rules to be grudgingly obeyed but as guidelines to follow in order to love deeper. Through love, the commandments draw us closer to God and to one another, while at the same time they provide us with personal protection and pleasure. Living for God and for others is to live a life of worship. Then, and only then, do things like prayer, church, Bible reading, and the commandments

---

[257] 1 Cor. 13:1-3, 13.

make any sense. They become expressions of a life of love and worship. As Paul wrote in Romans:

> *And so, dear brothers and sisters, I plead with you to give your bodies to God. Let them be a living and holy sacrifice—the kind he will accept. When you think of what he has done for you, is this too much to ask?*[258]

When Jesus saw the understanding of the teacher of the law, he didn't call him a heretic; instead, Jesus said, *"You are not far from the Kingdom of God."*[259]

"Love God and do as you please!"

"And after that, no one dared to ask him any more questions."[260]

---

[258] Rom. 12:1.

[259] Mark 12:34.

[260] Ibid.

Conclusion

There is no better way to conclude this book than to restate what was said in the introduction. God gave us these commandments for our protection and pleasure. He gave them to us so that we would be able to know *how* to love God and others. And he asked us to continually live and teach them so that they would become a part of us and so that succeeding generations would be able to see and know the ways of the Lord. In other words, he gave them to us because he truly is a *good* God. Moses' call to the people of his day is just as relevant for us today.

> *"Do not add to or subtract from these commands I am giving you from the LORD your God. Just obey them...."*
>
> *"You must obey these laws and regulations when you arrive in the land you are about to enter and occupy. The LORD my God gave them to me and commanded me to pass them on to you. If you obey them carefully, you will display your wisdom and intelligence to the surrounding nations. When they hear about these laws, they*

will exclaim, 'What other nation is as wise and prudent as this!' For what great nation has a god as near to them as the LORD our God is near to us whenever we call on him? And what great nation has laws and regulations as fair as this body of laws that I am giving you today?

"But watch out! Be very careful never to forget what you have seen the LORD do for you. Do not let these things escape from your mind as long as you live! And be sure to pass them on to your children and grand-children. Tell them especially about the day when you stood before the LORD your God at Mount Sinai, where he told me, 'Summon the people before me, and I will instruct them. That way, they will learn to fear me as long as they live, and they will be able to teach my laws to their children.' You came near and stood at the foot of the mountain, while the mountain was burning with fire. Flames shot into the sky, shrouded in black clouds and deep darkness. And the LORD spoke to you from the fire. You heard his words but didn't see his form; there was only a voice. He proclaimed his covenant, which he commanded you to keep—the Ten Commandments—and wrote them on two stone tablets."[261]

---

[261] Deut. 4:2, 6-13.

Bibliography

Arterburn, Stephen & Stoeker, Fred. *Every Man's Battle.* Colorado Springs, CO: WaterBrook, 2000.

Augustine. *Confessions,* II, v. 12.

Bakker, Jim. *I Was Wrong.* Nashville, TN: Nelsob, 1996.

Briscoe, Stuart. *The 10 Commandments.* Wheaton, IL: Harold Shaw, 1986.

Budge, E.A.W., *Tutankhamen.* New York, NY: Bell.

Byfield, Ted and Virginia. "Orthodoxy—Sometimes the Wealthy actually do Sell everything and give to the Poor." *Alberta Report,* Edmonton, AB: Oct. 26, 1998.

Byfield, Ted and Virginia. "Orthodoxy—While Liberal Clerics deplore Conversion, Jan Fonda and a Calgary Porn King defy them." *The Report.* Edmonton, AB, July 24, 2000.

Carroll, Lewis. *Alice's Adventures in Wonderland.*

Calvin, John. *Institutes of the Christian Religion.* Edited and translated by Henry Beveridge, Grand Rapids, MI: Eerdmans, 1997.

Calvin, John. *Ten Commandments.* Edited and translated by Benjamin Farley, Grand Rapids, MI: Baker, 1980.

Hoffman, Andrew. *Inventing Mark Twain.* New York, NY: Quill, 1997.

Jennison, Kate. "Interested? She's a present. From your suspicious wife: Wherever there is a hotel lobby, gentleman, chances are your wife can arrange for a decoy to 'test' you.' *National Post*. Tuesday, April 16, 2002.

Kung, Hans. *On Being A Christian*. Translator: Edward Quinn. Great Britain, Glasgow: Fount, 1978.

Leland, John. "Searching for a Holy Spirit: Young people are openly passionate about religion—but they insist on defining it in their own way." *Newsweek*. May 8, 2000.

Lewis, C.S. *Voyage of the Dawn Treader*. Canada: Fontana/Lions, 1952.

London H.B. & Wiseman, Neil B. *Pastors at Greater Risk*. Ventura, CA: Regal, 2003.

Luther, Martin. *Large Catechism*. Translated by J.N. Lenker. Minneapolis, MI: Augsburg, 1967.

Lutzer, Erwin. *How in the World can I be Holy?* Chicago, IL; Moody, 1974.

Morgan, Robert J. *On This Day*. Nashville, TN: Thomas Nelson, 1997.

Mother Teresa, *In My Own Words*. Compiled by Jose Luis Gonzalez-Balado, New York, NY: Gramercy, 1996.

Nouwen, Henri. *Creative Ministry*. USA: Image, 1978.

Reeves, Thomas. *The Empty Church*. New York, NY: Free Press, 1996.

Retief, Frank. *Divorce*. Cape Town, South Africa: Struik, 1990.

Rose, Roger. "Mad At The World—Boomerang." Song: *Isn't Sex A Wonderful Thing*. Santa Ana. CA; Alarma Records, Broken Songs, 1991.

Schaeffer, Francis. *The Mark of the Christian*. Downers Grove, IL: IVP, 1970.

Sweet, Leonard. *souLTsunami*. Grand Rapids, MI: Zondervan, 1999.

Templeton, Charles. *Farewell to God*. Toronto, ON: McClelland & Stewart, 1996.

Tolstoy, Leo. *How Much Land Does a Man Need?* Os Guinness (Ed), *Steering Through Chaos*. Colorado Springs, CO: NavPress, 2000.

Willard, Dallas. *The Divine Conspiracy*. New York, NY: HarperSanFrancisco, 1998.

"Just Gotta Have It!" *Edmonton Sun*. Mar. 19, 2001.

Holy Bible, New Living Translation. copyright © 1996 by Tyndale Charitable Trust.

Power 92 (92.5 FM) in Edmonton, AB, Canada.

"As dog as my witness...: Only in America: a bizarre court case over stolen 58 cents." *The Edmonton Journal*. Thursday, March 29, 2001.

Webster's New World Dictionary (1984).